A HOBBYIST'S
GUIDE TO
THEC64
MINI

Holger Weßling

Published in 2019 by
Acorn Books
www.acornbooks.co.uk

Typography and layout by
Andrews UK Limited
www.andrewsuk.com

Contents

Introduction

This book is the ultimate compendium to the THEC64 Mini, updated with the newest features from firmware V1.2.0.

It contains a large collection of tips and tricks for hardware, useful software and interesting internet links for the Mini. Retro Games has answered my every question and as a result, a lot of official answers went into this book.

You will learn about all new commands and features of the latest firmware. Learn to use and extend the Mini with a variety of new games compared to the possibilities you have using the original menu.

Many tools and tricks make loading new games from USB and by PC much easier with almost all Commodore file formats.

I found and interviewed dedicated users who took the Mini apart and analyzed the hardware. What gave birth from tinkering with the hardware is the information from which you now can benefit. For example, you can learn about the joystick and USB-Ports compatibilities, why delays can occur between a joystick action and the screen display and what you can do about it.

Learn to add own games and how to change the menu music, which seems easy at first, but is technically somehow more difficult to implement than you might think.

I do hope that you will find a lot of suggestions to revive or deepen your love for the C64 in this book and that you will have a lot of fun playing and experimenting.

1 Retro Games announcements

October 2018

On the USA Amazon site we are pleased to say on its day of release THEC64 mini has rocketed to the number one position in the category they placed it in for the whole of the USA! Massive thanks to everyone who has supported us by purchasing it, we hope you all enjoy it and we do appreciate your support, thank you

17 August 2018

It's been a good, productive summer here at Retro Games Ltd.

Now that the dust has settled from getting the US firmware release of THEC64 Mini out of the door, we've been spending some time on new firmware features for all regional models, most excitingly an easy-to-use disk management menu. The underlying technology has been completed, and we're now working on the user interface.

The screenshots here show an earlier version of the user interface to give you a taste of where it's heading. The second screenshot shows a new "disk access" icon which, when selected, reveals the disk menu shown in the third screenshot. Essentially this allows users to browse disk images on USB memory sticks, inserting a disk image or inserting and auto-running a disk image with optionally enabled fast-loading.

Once all of the testing is concluded here, these new features will be made available to all existing THEC64 owners via the official website.

23 July 2018

Retro Games Ltd. and Solutions 2 GO announced today that the THEC64® Mini is coming to North American retail stores on October 9, 2018. THEC64® Mini, a 50% replica of the of the world's bestselling home computer that launched in 1982, comes pre-loaded with 64 classic games and THEC64® Joystick. Originally designed with fans of the original machine in mind, THEC64® Mini is also attractive to kids and families thanks to its simple plug and play action. Aspiring gamers of yesteryear can revisit the

past and program their own games – just add a keyboard, and THEC64®
Mini becomes a fully functional home computer complete with C64 BASIC.

THEC64® Mini is available now for pre-order now at retailers across North
America.

"We are delighted to be able to bring back some of the most loved retro
games ever, on one of the most successful formats of all time", said Paul
Andrews, Retro Games' Managing Director. "The North American release
of THEC64® mini is a reimagining of the classic C64 computer and one of a
series of products we have on the way."

Check out the new trailer HERE: youtu.be/zs2W_-R75Dk

July 2018

THEC64 Mini targets the general public and is deliberately very simple to
use with very few options, and expects no knowledge or technical experience. We appreciate that it is also loved by active C64 enthusiasts who
wish to have the advanced features they are used to using.

We would therefore like THEC64 to provide additional features for advanced users. However, because they are not the main users of the THEC64,
we have to be very careful to balance additional features against the needs
of the general public so that we do not compromise THEC64's ease of use.

Now that people are using the THEC64 we are considering the feedback,
and building things into our development plan, but any changes must fit
into our existing tight development schedule, so we are looking at new
features when we can as time permits.

Advanced users have asked for additional program loading features, so
this is something we are currently looking at. At this stage we cannot give
a timeline on this feature because the team is focusing on the US release.

6 July 2018

We are pleased to confirm one of the great new games coming your way in
due course, for you to be able to add for free, to your THEC64 via a pending
firmware update will be…

Galencia - Galencia is a retro inspired shoot 'em up, described by various
reviewers as –

"smooth slick and totally addictive. A sure fire sizzler in my book" – JR

"the most polished C64 release I have seen in 2017. Strongly recommended"

"the best 'galaga' game I have seen on the C64, it is absolutely fantastic" – Sprite Castle

Here is an online video of the game action –

https://youtu.be/oA5Hwr6SFJg

Full details of the final version heading your way will be posted very soon, but for now, here are some of the details of the games current version.

50 Action Packed Levels

Asteroid Fields

Challenging Stages

Boss Battles

Ebb and Flow difficulty curve

Siren enemy with Tractor beam for Double Ship Action

Introduction, Launch and Completion sequences

6 Brand new SID tunes, unique to this project

This game will be added to a pending firmware release for all owners to update their machine, and in the process add this game to their THEC64 console! Full details soon.

29 June 2018

Just a small update this week, as we have been hard at work on getting the 'mystery games' ready to give to you guys. We are working on the best way to add them into one of the pending firmware updates heading your way as soon as we can. We want to allow even a casual user the opportunity to add the bonus free games to their THEC64 mini consoles easily and quickly. Hence we are looking at the best way to add them by incorporating them into a firmware update, (which will of course also have other improvements added into that firmware update as well).

In other small ongoing news, work and testing is still moving forward on future regional releases, future hardware releases, and future software and firmware releases in general, so have no fear we are hard at work here! This is an ongoing project/company we are not going anywhere, and have an ongoing internal program planned.

Again, see you all next week, and let's see what we can hopefully reveal in more detail by then!

22 June 2018

Tomorrow is the 'Celebration of the life of Rick Dickinson' ceremony, and so today, as our own small tribute to one of the nicest humans we have ever met, someone who created some of the most iconic designs of our lifetime, and someone we are proud to have called a friend, we present a few images he created and then shared with us back in 2016.

Rick shared these images with us privately, as having worked with him in the past, and being massive fans of his work, and also having the privilege to share some social time with him, he created these initial concept renders, and sent them to us. For multiple reasons, we decided it was inappropriate to work with Rick on what would in time become THEC64 range, and even though we did not contract/pay Rick to do any work on the range, and we never actually used any of his designs or concepts, nothing could stop him from creating, and nothing could stop him from teasing us with these concepts on his take, on what would become in due course THEC64.

We would like to extend to Rick's family our condolences and sorrow at their loss, and also our best wishes to them also, and hope that they, and others, DO celebrate the life of Rick Dickinson at the event tomorrow.

Thank you for everything you gave us all Rick, and we hope everyone likes this glimpse of what might have been that you kindly shared with us, and now we are sharing with the rest of the world.

Rick Dickinson : 1956 – 2018 (industrial designer)

You can find our news here https://thec64.com/news/

2 Update / upgrade firmware

Your very first step should be to upgrade the firmware of your Mini. This will make everything much easier for you!

Attention! You cannot install a firmware that is older than the build version currently installed!

E.g. you can't install the V1.0.7 when V1.0.8 already is installed. You can only download and install more recent versions.

> **Question:** Why can't the firmware be downgraded? Will this be possible in the future?

> **Retro Games:** Being able to downgrade firmware would make the upgraded user interface much more complicated. For users to be confident in what they are doing, Retro Games made the procedure and user interface as simple as possible. The Mini detects the most recent upgrade on the USB stick and tries to install this version.

The official link: https://thec64.com/upgrade/

2.1 How to upgrade
See also: 5.1 USB sticks

Firmware Version 1.1.0 and above:

The upgrade file will automatically detect which firmware THEC64 Mini is running on and will install the appropriate upgrade version for you, hassle-free.

To see the new USB File Loader in action, watch the official video via the provided link: https://youtu.be/iXmIyNpJxNM

What is in the video?

"Insert an USB stick and use the joystick to browse the content. If you need to, turn off the Fastloader option by pressing button C on the joystick and then press fire to load the file. You can configure programs on a file-by-file basis, adjusting loading speeds, machine types, mapping joystick buttons and much more, or you can choose to use THEC64 Mini's default settings."

This is the official Guide on how to upgrade the Mini:

1. Check the current firmware version on the Mini by selecting the SYSTEM icon from OPTIONS on the HOME screen and then choose System information from the menu. Look for the Build version (e.g. theC64-1.0.1-argent).

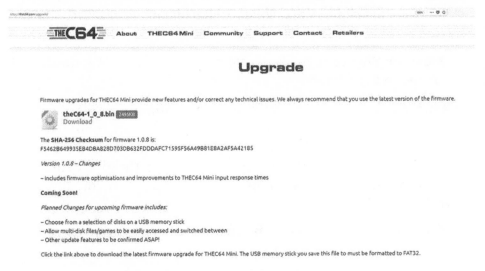

2. Check that the latest version is newer than the version installed on your Mini.

3. Download the latest firmware file here https://thec64.com/upgrade/ and save the file (e.g. theC64-1_0_8.bin) to your USB memory stick. Do not place the file inside a folder on the stick or rename the file. If you do, the Mini will not find the upgrade.

4. Insert the USB memory stick into an unoccupied USB port on the Mini.

5. Ensure that you have the Mini joystick or an alternative controller connected to another USB port.

6. Select the SYSTEM icon from OPTIONS on the HOME screen on the Mini and choose System Information.

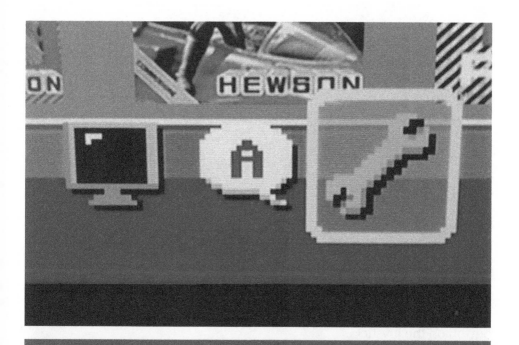

USB keyboard ›

Legal notices ›

System information ›

Factory reset ›

7. The upgrade file will now be detected and you are asked to close or apply.

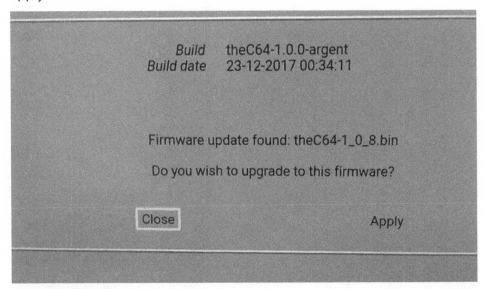

Build   theC64-1.0.0-argent
Build date   23-12-2017 00:34:11

Firmware update found: theC64-1_0_8.bin

Do you wish to upgrade to this firmware?

Close   Apply

8. If you choose apply, then the upgrade begins. If you choose not to upgrade at this time, select Close and press FIRE, or simply press the MENU button on the joystick.

9. After a successful upgrade, your Mini will shut down and restart automatically.

10. You can check the firmware version afterwards by following point (1) above.

2.1.1 YouTube: How to update firmware from 1.0.1 up to 1.0.8

If you search on YouTube for "THEC64 Mini - How to update firmware 1.0.6 & 1.0.7 | Quick & Easy Guide [Commodore 64] C64", you will find a video that shows you how to upgrade your Mini.

Of course, this also applies for other firmware versions: https://www.youtube.com/watch?v=lrHkWHHv7cY

2.2 Firmware – Bug fixes etc. – History & changes

Planned changes for upcoming firmware include:
– Choose from a selection of disks on an USB memory stick
– Allow multi-disk files/games to be easily accessed and switched between
– Other update features to be confirmed ASAP!

The changes so far:

1.2.0 – Adds a completely new game for free to the GAMES CAROUSEL! Galencia https://retrogames.biz/thec64-mini/games for the Mini is licensed from Jay Aldred and is the winner of the Reset64 Magazine 2017 Commodore 64 Game of the Year Award
– Introduces the Virtual Joystick. You can now select all options on THEC64 Mini and even play games just using a USB keyboard. See Virtual Joystick for further information
– Improves the File Loader to allow multiple programs to be configured at once. See Setting a Default Configuration for Multiple Programs for further information
– Remembers the mute state of the CAROUSEL music between reboots
– Improves the general performance of THEC64 Mini screens and menus

Galencia is the winner of the Reset64 Magazine 2017 Commodore 64 Game of the Year Award. It is a colourful, highly polished, Galaga inspired single-screen shoot-em-up.

Jay has worked really hard to produce a special version of Galencia just for THEC64 Mini and its 720p display, and it makes maximum use of the upper and lower borders for graphics, right up to the edge of the screen! Be aware however, that some HD TVs might crop some of these border graphics when displaying the 720p image. This is not a fault with Galencia or the Mini and we recommend that you refer to your TV settings.

1.1.4 – Corrects a recent firmware issue that prevented joysticks like the Logitech F710 from being detected

1.1.2 – Fixes an issue where some USB directory layouts result in an empty file list

1.1.1 – Corrected USB behavior that helps resolve issues users experienced with some USB memory sticks when using the File Loader

1.1.0 – Introduced the File Loader so that compatible programs can be loaded from USB.
– Fixes a small issue with the German virtual keyboard
– Adds the in-game help function in 'Avenger' to button A on the joystick
– Includes various firmware optimizations and enhancements.

1.0.8 – Includes firmware optimizations and improvements to THEC64 Mini input response times

1.0.7 – Fixes an issue encountered on some two-player games when using two USB joysticks

1.0.6 – Maps additional functions to joystick buttons for some games
– Makes minor changes to descriptions for some games
– Fixes an occasional scenario where an additional USB joystick is not detected until a restart
– Fixes an irregular audio click when opening the THEC64 Mini's MENU in-Game

Version 1.0.1 to 1.0.5 were internal revisions and are not released. The release notes for 1.0.6 are the changes between 1.0.0 and 1.0.6.

This link https://thec64.com/upgrade-archive/ will lead you to the Upgrade Archive.

3 Software

Question: Originally the Mini was announced with Sam's Journey to be free along with the Mini, as the original indiegogo campaign page shows. What happened to this?

Retro Games: This was the hope for the original crowdfunding of the full sized version. Retro Games is still in contact with the creators of Sam's Journey and while it is not currently on THEC64 Mini, potentially, they hope it might be on other versions or options of the THEC64 as the range grows.

3.1 File Loader for firmware v1.1.0 and above

Using the File Loader function and a FAT32 formatted USB memory stick, THEC64 Mini loads programs from various C64 file formats. Supported file formats include:

Disk images: D64, G64, D81, D82
Tape image file: T64, TAP
Others: PRG, P00 and CRT

To make file browsing and selection less arduous, the File Loader currently has a display limit of 256 files and/or folders per-folder, including the root of the memory stick. This equates to 18 pages of listed items to navigate through with your joystick.

Please note that only C64 programs supplied by Retro Games Ltd for use on THEC64 Mini are covered by the Warranty. This does not affect your statutory rights. Please read the Warranty https://retrogames. biz/support/warranty/ for further details.

Control how THEC64 Mini configures a program loaded from a USB memory stick in two ways:

• Add specific flags to the filename, or
• Create a CJM text configuration file for each program file

Either method gives THEC64 Mini information used to load and run a program correctly from USB. Note that some programs will load and run correctly just using the default settings, explained below.

Default settings

In the absence of flags in filenames or CJM text configuration files, THEC64 Mini applies default settings to any supported file it finds on a USB memory stick:

- THEC64 Mini uses a fast loader to speed up loading times
- THEC64 Mini also uses faster disk access (but only for disk image files)
- The primary joystick is set to port 2. The secondary joystick is set to port 1 only if a second joystick is connected before loading the program from USB
- The type of C64 chosen to load the program is automatically based upon whether THEC64 Mini firmware is North American (an NTSC C64 is chosen) or European (a PAL C64 is chosen). This does not affect the HDMI output
- No program functions map to the joystick buttons other than the standard directions and the FIRE and MENU buttons

Many programs load and run fine using the default settings. If your program does not, or you wish to change the configuration, please refer to **Appendix A**.

The File Loader

Whilst on the HOME screen, insert a USB memory stick that contains supported C64 files into an available USB port on THEC64 Mini. After a few seconds, an icon appears beneath the GAMES CAROUSEL to confirm the USB memory stick is connected.

Highlight the USB icon and press FIRE. The FILE LOADER screen lists any supported files and folders stored in the root of the USB memory stick.

Note that file extensions (for example: D64, TAP, CRT), flags added to filenames (for example _TP) and CJM files (for example, c64-disk. cjm) are NOT shown in the list.

Highlight a file and press FIRE. The selected file loads and runs. How long it takes to load will vary based upon the type of file and the settings used by THEC64 Mini to load it.

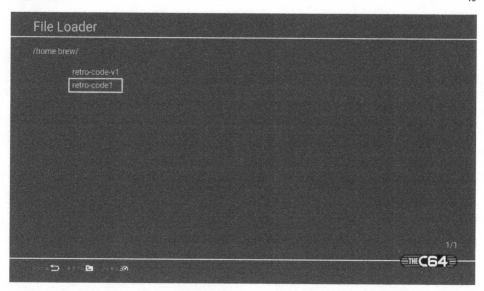

Move the highlight over a folder and press FIRE. The contents of the sub-folder appear. You cannot enter a folder that is empty or does not contain any other folders or supported C64 files.

When inside a folder on the USB memory stick, press button A on the joystick to move out of the current folder. Alternatively, push LEFT to come out of a folder when on the far left side of the File Loader list.

The C64 Fast Loader is switched on by default, speeding up loading times. For those programs that do not load if the fast loader is ON, press button C on the joystick (a red X appears over the Fast Loader icon) before you press FIRE to load. This turns the fast loader OFF.

Note that the faster disk access function remains ON unless you specifically turn it OFF via filename flags or a CJM file. See Appendix A for full details.

Save/Load from USB

When loading a program file from a USB memory stick, the Save/Load function saves and loads on the USB memory stick rather than on THEC64 Mini. You have four slots to save to per program.

Save files are stored inside a folder on the USB memory stick called "THEC64SAVE". Inside that folder are sub-folders that contain your saves.

For example THEC64SAVES\c64-disk\ contains saved files for a C64 disk image file called 'c64-disk'.

BASIC and accessing a USB memory stick

Please note that the only file stored on a USB stick that can be loaded directly when running BASIC on THEC64 Mini is a disk image with the filename THEC64-drive8.d64. Please visit programming-in-c64-basic https:// retrogames.biz/support/programming-in-c64-basic/ and the faq https:// retrogames.biz/support/faq/ for further details on BASIC and THEC64-drive8.d64 file.

APPENDIX A – CONFIGURING C64 PROGRAMS

Add flags to each filename

By adding flags to the end of the filename, you define which joystick port(s) are used, specify the machine type (PAL or NTSC), set a disk to be read-only, turn on accurate disk loading (for troublesome disk image files that won't load quickly), and disable the on-screen disk icon.

For example, the program on a disk image file called 'c64-disk.d64' requires a joystick connected to port 1 on the original C64 computer. Rename your d64 file 'c64-disk_J1.d64'.

Below is a list of all the available flags:

J1   This sets the primary joystick port as port 1. With a second Joystick connected, it automatically uses port 2

J2   This sets the primary joystick port as port 2. With a second Joystick connected, it automatically uses port 1. Note that port 2 is the default set by THEC64 Mini, so it doesn't *have* to be specified by this flag

AD   This flag turns 'accurate disk drive' mode on (for original slower disk loading) and turns off the fastdisk mode which is ON by default

RO   This makes the disk appear as read-only (which prevents THEC64 Mini writing to the disk image)

NI   This flag disables the drive icon from appearing on-screen during disk loading

TN   This runs as an NTSC C64. It doesn't affect the HDMI output

TP   This runs as a PAL C64. It doesn't affect the HDMI output

Add flags to the end of the filename in any order. For example:

c64-disk_TNROJ1.d64 or
c64-disk_ROJ1TN.d64 or
c64-disk_J1TNRO.d64

Create a CJM file for each program file

Using a computer that can create new files, create a text file on the USB memory stick that includes joystick port requirements, machine type (PAL or NTSC) settings, accurate disk loading options, additional joystick button mappings and other settings for each program file.

You can use the standard text editors that come with Windows, Linux and Mac OS to create CJM files. Ensure that your file does end with a .cjm file extension, otherwise it will not be recognised by THEC64 Mini. For those who are interested, the files needs to be UTF-8 or ASCII encoded and must not contain any non-standard characters.

Save the CJM text file in the same folder as the program file on your USB stick. For example, 'c64-disk.d64' has a corresponding file 'c64-disk.cjm'.

THEC64 Mini always uses a CJM file in preference to any filename flags or default settings.

An example CJM file looks like this:

```
X:pal,accuratedisk,driveicon
J:2*:JU,JD,JL,JR,JF,JF,SP,1,SP,2,3,4,JF
J:1:JU,JD,JL,JR,JF,JF,JF,JF,JF,,,,JF
V:12
```

As you can see from the example given, each line in a CJM text file complies with the following:

```
type: value [,value]
```

Entity name	Entity type	Values	Description
Computer configuration	X	pal ntsc driveicon readonly accuratedisk	This sets the parameters needed to configure the C64 computer before it loads and runs the program.
			The values are case sensitive and must be in lower case.
			pal – This makes the program behave as though running on a European (PAL) C64. It doesn't affect the HDMI output of THEC64 Mini.
			ntsc – This makes the program behave as though running on a North American (NTSC) C64. It doesn't affect the HDMI output of THEC64 Mini.
			driveicon – This activates the on-screen drive icon, to show when a disk is accessed.
			readonly – This makes a disk read-only, meaning THEC64 Mini cannot write back to the disk.
			accuratedisk – This switches ON accurate (slower) disk drive functionality, necessary for some programs to load correctly. This is off by default.
Vertical display shift	V	-16 to +16	This number moves the screen position up or down over a range of + or – 16 display lines (pal). This is useful if a game has graphics that appear in the top or bottom border, as an HDMI 720p television screen can otherwise clip them. For ntsc programs, going above +7 or +8 could exhibit display problems at the bottom of the screen.

Entity name	Entity type	Values	Description
Joystick configuration	J	See follow- ing table for allowed values	

Note that the entity type is always a capital letter rather than a lower case, e.g. an X rather than an x, otherwise THEC64 Mini will ignore the entity type and the values associated with it in the CJM file.

Joystick configuration consists of 13 values that define how the joystick is to operate in the program.

The first value (after the J: entity) defines the primary port (1 or 2, with primary indicated by an *), followed by what happens when the joystick is pushed UP, DOWN, LEFT or RIGHT. The next two values define what happens when the LEFT FIRE and RIGHT FIRE buttons are pressed. The next two values define what happens when the TL and TR triangle buttons are pressed. The next value is an extra joystick button (not available on THEC64 Mini Joystick) but it usually assigned the same value as the TR button. The next three values are buttons A, B and C on THEC64 Joystick. The final value is another button not available on THEC64 Joystick, but is usually assigned the same value as the TL button. For example:

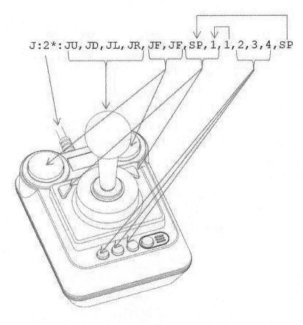

In the shown example, the joystick is behaving as if connected to port 2 on the original C64 computer. Moving up, down, left and right using the stick is as you would expect. Both FIRE buttons perform the same joystick fire (JF) function. Pressing TL on the joystick is the same as pressing the Spacebar (SP). Pressing TR is the same as pressing the 1 key, and buttons A, B and C do the same job as pressing keys 2, 3 and 4 respectively.

Joystick parameters are the port assignments first, then the joystick stand-ard functions, then the button mapping:

Joystick to key map ID	Description
JU JD JL JR JF	Joystick directions Up, Down, Left, Right and Fire
F1 F2 F3 F4 F5 F6 F7 F8	C64 function keys F1 to F8
AL	Arrow Left
AU	Arrow Up
CM	C64 key
CO	Comma
CT	Control
CU	Cursor Up
CD	Cursor Down
CL	Cursor Left
CR	Cursor Right
DL	Delete
EN	Return
HM	Home
RS	RUN/STOP
RE	RESTORE
SL	SHIFT Left

Joystick to key map ID	Description
SR	SHIFT Right
SS	SHIFT Lock
SP	Spacebar
PO	Pound (£)

Assigning letters and numbers to joystick buttons is easy. For example, to assign pressing key A to a Joystick button, just enter A in the CJM data for the relevant button.

Considerations

In all of the games provided with THEC64 Mini, the LEFT and RIGHT joystick FIRE buttons have the same function (JF) so both left and right-handed players can use either button as FIRE. However, the LEFT and RIGHT joystick FIRE buttons are independent, so you can assign one FIRE button to JF and the other to a different function if you wish in your CJM files.

In addition, for consistency all of the games on the GAMES CAROUSEL start by pressing TL or by pressing a FIRE button. If you wish to retain this logic, keep in mind how your program starts once it has finished loading when you assign joystick buttons in the CJM file. If FIRE does not start the program, then assign the appropriate key press to the TL button.

3.2 Setting a Default Configuration for Multiple Programs

For firmware 1.2.0 and above

Please read the guidance on using the File Loader before you read the following additional instructions for enhancements to the use of CJM files:

THEC64 Mini allows you to override the settings that the Mini applies to a program loaded from a USB stick through either filename flags, or a C64 Joystick Map (CJM) file. Starting with firmware 1.2.0, you can provide default settings for all files within a folder. This is particularly useful if you have multiple files that you wish to apply the same settings for.

Creating a default configuration for a folder

To configure programs within a folder, you create a CJM file in exactly the same way you would if you were configuring an individual program and place it in the folder with the special filename THEC64-default.cjm

If present, THEC64 Mini will use this CJM configuration whenever there is no file-specific CJM file for the program being loaded.

An important and useful point to note is that THEC64 Mini will apply the settings supplied by a thec64-default.cjm file to all programs within the folder in which it is placed, even if the programs are in sub-folders.

How THEC64 Mini applies settings

THEC64 Mini will apply settings in the following order:

1. If a CJM file is present for the program being loaded from a USB stick, its settings are applied;

2. Otherwise, if a default CJM file is present in the folder containing the program (or one of its parent folders) then those settings are applied;

3. Otherwise, any filename flags present at the end of the program filename are applied as settings;

4. Otherwise, the built-in THEC64 Mini settings are applied to the program.

Structuring your files and folders on the USB stick

The folder level configuration feature works best when your C64 files and folders are arranged in a logical order on the USB memory stick. For example:

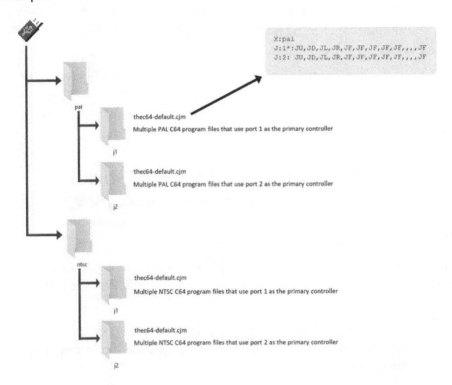

The content of the file is the same as you would expect from any other cjm file used by THEC64 Mini. For example, in the above \pal\j1 folder is thec64-default.cjm:

```
X:pal
J:1*:JU,JD,JL,JR,JF,JF,JF,JF,JF,,,,JF
J:2:  JU,JD,JL,JR,JF,JF,JF,JF,JF,,,,JF
```

Every program stored in that folder will run on a PAL C64, and use Joystick port 1 as the primary controller.

If THEC64 Mini doesn't find thec64-default.cjm file in the folder, then it comes out of the current folder and looks in the parent folder instead. It continues to behave this way, working its way back up the folder structure until it reaches the root of the USB memory stick.

If it doesn't find thec64-default.cjm file then it will run the currently se-lected C64 program file based upon an individually named cjm file, or by filename flags as you would expect. As a last resort it will apply the system default settings, which are joystick 2 as the primary port and either PAL or NTSC (based upon if THEC64 Mini is a European or North American model, respectively).

Note: If you need different settings for each C64 program file (e.g. joystick buttons, vertical shift and so on), then use the standard cjm method, nam-ing the cjm file after the individual C64 program file rather than using this alternative default method.

3.3 Program start from USB stick

Insert a USB stick with your favourite game on it into the Mini. You can easily start it by clicking on the USB symbol in the Mini's main menu and select your game in the following menu.

Only with firmware version 1.1.0 or higher you can start a program (.prg) directly from an USB stick without having to rename it first like with older firmware versions.

However, there are combinations of letters and special characters that the Mini cannot interpret. Therefore, it is better to use only numbers and let-ters for a file name.

If the game does not start, it can be due to the built-in Fastloader of the Mini.

Try the procedure above again before you click on the game, press the button C on the Mini-Joystick to switch off the Fastloader. Then start the game.

If you select a .d64 file, the first program in the file will start automatically. If another program of the .d64 file is to be started, you must first start BASIC and list the directory.

- Insert the USB stick into the Mini.

- Go to the carousel mode (the first menu in which the games are selected or the start screen) and select BASIC.

- In BASIC type LOAD"$",8 to get a list of the drive.

- Then type LIST and click Enter to display the list.

- Type LOAD"program name",8,1 to load the program.

- Then type RUN and click ENTER to start the program.

Firmware older than 1.1.0?

Up to firmware 1.0.8, the image from which the Mini should start must always have the name "THEC64-drive8.d64". Thus, each image must be renamed by typed in manually so that the Mini recognizes the image. You will find more about this in the next chapter.

3.4 USB disk management

Here you will find tools with which you can handle all file and directory operations for the Mini.

Since firmware 1.1.0, you can build directories on an USB-stick and sort your programs in those folders.

More than 256 files are not supported by the Mini!

3.4.1 DirMaster

See also: 10.2 More games

DirMaster is a 32-bit Windows program (that also runs under 64-bit) with which you can create your own D64 images, program and Game collections.

Through this link you can download the newest version: http://style64. org/release/dirmaster-v3.1.1-style

Here, you can find some videos showing how the program works (open youtube.com and search for "DirMaster" or use this link:

https://www.youtube.com/results?search_query=dirmaster

It is also excellent for converting between different disk formats.

DirMaster supports common (and uncommon) emulator disk-image-formats (such as .d64, .d81, .d2m, etc.), almost every native Commodore archival format (such as .arc, .sda, .lnx, etc.) and many native graphic formats (such as koala, doodle, amica, etc.). DirMaster was designed to give users a perfect blend of a familiar appearance (e.g. natural looking disk-image contents using the PETSCII character set) and modern GUI functionality (e.g. drag and drop, opening multiple disk images at once). The first version of DirMaster was released in 2006.

Features

- Disk-image support: .d64, .d71, .d81, .d80, .d82, .d2m, .d4m, .dhd, .hdd (read-only), .dnp, .dfi, .m2i (read-only), .t64, .g64 (read-only), .nib (read-only)

- file support: .prg/.p00, .seq/.s00, .usr/.u00, .rel/.r00

- archive support: .arc, .sda, .lnx, .sfx, .ark, .lbr, .spy, .cvt, .wr3, zip/4 (1!..., 2!..., etc.)

- integrated with Explorer via file associations/icons

- integrated with the Windows Explorer file preview panel

- all the usual directory editing capabilities like sorting, block size change/correction, file type change, lock, splat, etc.

- most functions activated by keyboard equivalents, including file reordering and filename editing

- multi-level undo

- pervasive drag and drop:
  - copy one or more files from one image to another
  - copy files between different image formats (e.g. d64 to d81, dfi to d71, etc.)

- move/reorder files on the same disk by dragging them

  - drag and drop files from disk images to the OS file system

  - drag and drop files from the file system onto disk images

- multi selection with shift+click & ctrl+click; many operations will work on the entire selection

- invoke your favourite emulator or other external application (up to eight slots) from within DirMaster to run/process a file or disk

- sub directory and partition support for relevant formats (d81, d2m, d4m, dnp)

- save disk images as a .txt, .csv (with optional MD5 hash per file), .bmp, .png, .rtf. and .html

- visual BAM mode with track/sector view/edit (hex and PETSCII)

- support for the most common error and extended disk extensions

- decompress archives directly from open disk images with one key click

- support for GEOS file types (new: GeoPaint/GeoPhotoAlbum viewers, GeoWrite to seq conversion)

- built in viewers for Commodore file types including raw binary (disassembly and hex viewers), SEQ files, REL files, BASIC listings (v2.0 and v7.0), character sets and many popular image formats

- recursive find: search your disk-image collection with * and ? wildcards; save results to a file

- batch processing: recursively create .txt, .csv, .bmp, .png, .rtf. and .html or extract to prg/seq files

- batch processing: send extracted files to an external script/executable

- experimental OpenCBM support http://opencbm.sourceforge.net/

- print directory listings for disk envelopes; two-sided directory printing

- maintain your own favourite 'separators': drag and drop them onto your disk-image

- disk forensics:

- check for cross links

- list the sector chain for each file, as well as a list of free chains (potentially recoverable deleted files)

- compare two disks at a sector by sector level

- customizable palettes; defaults to the "Pepto" palette but can use any .vpl (VICE) format palette file

3.4.2 MiniMount (only for firmware 1.0.8 or older)

MiniMount is a small utility, for Windows and AROS that helps to mount a disk-image file into the Mini by an USB drive.

Download: http://vmwaros.blogspot.com/p/minimount-for-c64-mini.html

The AROS Version is for Amiga and Amiga-like operating systems.

How to Use It
1. Format the USB drive as FAT32 with MBR (see 5.1 USB sticks).
2. Download MiniMount and extract it in the root of the USB drive. The MiniMount script file must be in the root directory of that drive!
3. Create a directory on the drive and copy all the .d64, .d71 or .d8* files you like to use to this location.
4. Run the MiniMount script by clicking twice on its icon.
5. Use the file requester, locate the image file of the game, select it and wait for a second or two.
6. Now the file has been copied to the root of the USB drive, together with the right naming.
7. Put the USB drive into your Mini when it is in carousel mode (The first menu where you select the games) and choose BASIC.
8. LOAD"$",8 to get a listing of the drive and write LOAD"program name",8,1 to load the program.
9. When you're done or want to "change disk", unplug the USB drive from the Mini and plug it back into your PC.
10. Repeat from Step 4.

3.4.3 THEC64 Disker (only for firmware 1.0.8 or older)

THEC64 Disker is a simple "THEC64 Mini" USB disk swap utility that makes setting the C64 BASIC default disk image easier.

Instructions

Using the software should almost be self-explanatory.

- Prepare an USB stick according to the Mini preparation instructions #1.

- Copy your d64 disk images to the USB stick. The files do not necessarily need to be in the root because Disker will perform a full subdirectory search for d64 files.

- Download the latest archive from https://github.com/prof79/ TheC64Disker/releases.

- Extract the archive to the root of your USB stick. The archive contains/ will automatically create a folder TheC64Disker in your USB stick root.

- After launching the program (TheC64Disker\TheC64Disker.exe), it will show you all disk images found on the USB stick. Click Activate to set any image as your THEC64-drive8.d64 image.

- Your original d64 file will not be changed or altered in any way :-)

- Using hashing technology, the program will tell you the currently active image if applicable. The active image will be shown in bold text.

- If THEC64-drive8.d64 already exists, you will be asked for permission to overwrite it. There is currently no backup function. Copy/rename it manually if there is data from the Mini BASIC mode you want to preserve.

- For an improved overall experience, you may consider using an AutoRun.inf file or creating an application shortcut in the USB stick root for easy access.

System Requirements

This application is based on Microsoft .NET and WPF technology. Due to the WPF requirement it is a Windows-only GUI tool.

The required .NET Framework version is 4.5.2.

For operating system support and pre-installed version guidance see .NET Framework system requirements. It should work from Windows Vista SP2 and Windows 7 SP1 onwards.

3.4.4 TheC64Copy (only for firmware 1.0.8 or older)

This is a simple windows application to copy Games from any folder onto an USB drive which then corrects the name to THEC64-drive8.d64.

You can choose which file format it should be (.d64 .d81 .d82).

To use a .d81 file, please open and close the Avenger game first (This maybe is fixed with a later firmware)

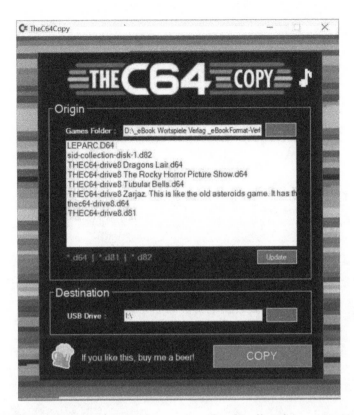

If you like to get in touch with the author for feedback or questions, go to Max http://thec64community.online/user/127 and send him a message.

The program requires .NET Framework 4.0 which you can download here from Microsoft: https://www.microsoft.com/en-US/Download/con-firmation.aspx?id=17718

3.5 Directory / listing

These tools act like an Explorer for files and directories. It also offers basic and expanded functionalities to deal with them.

First, put them in a disk image together with the game files and start it. Then, you can call all games in a listing.

TIP: Start automatically with a FileBrowser and Fastloader:

• Open DirMaster or a similar program

• Make a new .d64 image with Disk/New/D64

- Open in DirMaster one of the tools like CBM-Filebowser.d64

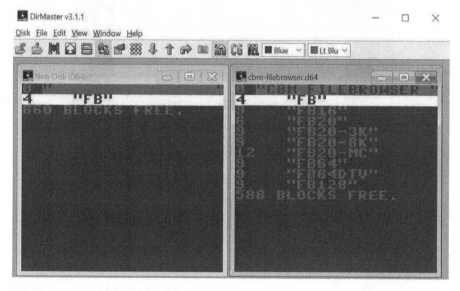

- Copy the main program (at CBM-FileBrowser this is the file "FB") into the empty D64

- Save the new image as .d64 (Only necessary firmware older 1.1.0 filename must be THEC64-drive8.d64) onto the USB-Drive and stick it into the Mini

- Start the Mini

- From the carousel load Allycat

- Exit the game

- From the carousel load BASIC

- From BASIC load the file FB with LOAD"FB",8,1

- Type RUN and push Enter

- Now make a save game

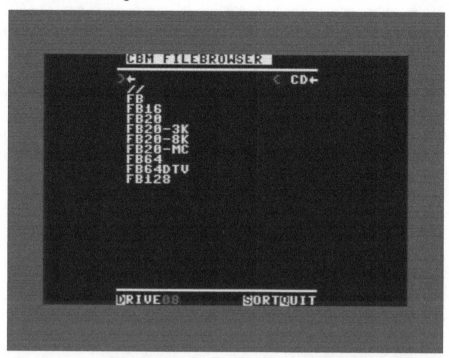

Now you have a nice disk menu every time you load in BASIC in save game.

Before you can use another disk image, you have to restart the Mini. Otherwise, the new image will not be recognized and the list will only show the entry with the FileBrowser.

After you start BASIC again, all you have to now is refresh the disk image.

In this way you are ready to handle all your .d64, .d81 and .d82 images.

3.5.1 C64 FIBR

FIBR is a file browser for the C64 and displays the directories of original Commodore floppies, SD2IEC (MMC2IEC) and MMC64. FIBR can also display the directories (e.g. hard disk images) of the emulators VICE and Power64 (also case-sensitive).

Our goal is to support most common card readers and hard disk interfaces in the future.

The browser is completely programmed in assembler and is extremely fast and compatible. It supports long file names, directories and D64 images. FIBR has a specially designed interface with a modified character set and (in a later version) selectable color themes.

The design is very clear and functional, the font is easy to read. The letters are smaller than normal C64 characters to increase the line spacing for better readability. You can switch between different views (1 window or 2 windows horizontally or vertically) and jump between the windows using the control key. There is a proportional scroll bar and names that are too long are neatly shortened.

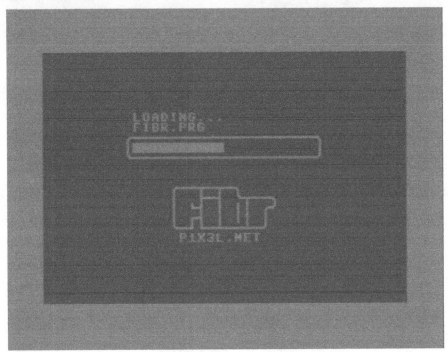

FIBR by P1X3Lnet Download: https://csdb.dk/release/?id=162390

3.5.2 CBM FileBrowser v1.6

CBM-FileBrowser is a program launcher for Commodore machines. Originally it was intended for sd2iec devices, but it works great with any CBM drive.

The archive has versions for the VIC20, C16, C128 and C64 including source and docs.

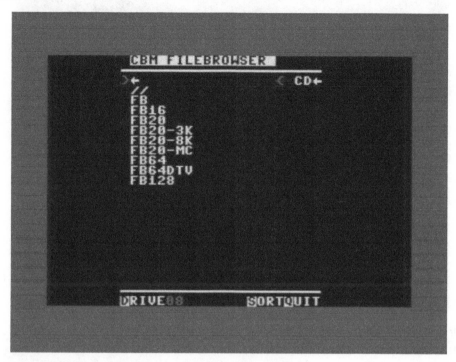

CBM FileBrowser by nbla000 (nbla000@gmail.com)

Download: http://commodore.software/index.
php?option=com_jdownloads&view=download&id=1140:c
bm-filebrowser-v1-6&catid=29&Itemid=126

3.5.3 SDBrowse V.697

Programmed by Michal Okowicki

It is not just for SD-Cards.

On YouTube you will find an introduction: https://youtu.be/Di7XkxjUxQI
Download: https://csdb.dk/release/?id=152470

3.6 Disk management

3.6.1 C64-Archiv

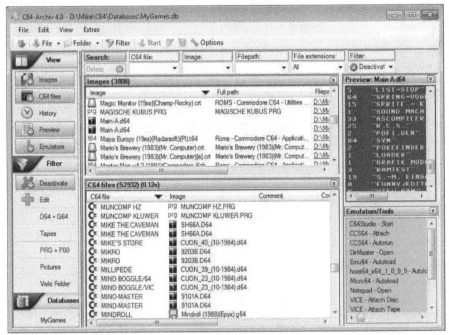

The C46 Archive program scans and stores your C64 collection (files, screenshots, documents, media files…)

File manager and disk viewer

Fast database to handle a huge number of files (> 1.000.000)

Starts C64 images and programs in these emulators: VICE, CCS64, HOXS64, EMU64 and MICRO64

Works with tools e.g.: C64Studio, C4Copy, D64Lister, DirMaster…

Stores C64 files: D64, D71, D81, G64, P00, PRG, T64, TAP and CRT

Stores emulator files: VSF (VICE-snapshot-file), VFL (VICE-Flipfile) and C64 (CCS64-session-file)

Stores picture files: BMP, GIF, JPG, PNG and TIFF

Stores media files: MP3, MP4 and AVI

Stores text and information files: PDF, TXT, NFO and DIZ

Searches within archive files: 7Z, ZIP and RAR

Available languages: English, Spanish and German

Download at: http://www.purmike.de/documents/c64archiv_en.html

From author Michael Rupp: In the spring of 1985, at the age of 13, I saw a C64 for the first time and was immediately hooked. To be able to raise the price of almost 600 DM, I increasingly delivered brochures to friends with half the payment. On Christmas 1985, I finally had the C64 in my hands. First, I programmed small BASIC games before I quickly created larger projects like a Sprite Editor or Adventures with Assembler. I still have the C64. In the meantime, after I had transferred the floppy disks to the PC, I still lacked the suitable program to manage the floppy disks. This gave rise to the idea of programming the C64 archive.

3.6.2 64Copy

64COPY is a universal DOS and C64 file manager modeled on the Norton Commander running under MS-DOS.

This means that 64COPY only runs in up to 32-bit DOS Environment (not 64-bit compatible).

It specializes in converting and manipulating emulator files between different formats. It also has a very flexible 6502 Disassembler. 64COPY does not communicate with the 1541/71/81 floppy disk drives to read floppy disks.

64COPY includes, among other things:

- File conversion between D64 (all types, including the F64 variant), D71, D81, D80, D82, DNP, D2M, T64, G64, ZipCode (all types), PC64 (Pxx, Sxx, Uxx, Rxx), LNX, DOS binaries, ARC, CRT, SDA, X64, LBR, ARK, SPY and CPK files.
- A very powerful 6502 Disassembler
- TEXT, HEX and D64 HEX editors
- FILE Viewer
- BASIC Unlister

- D64, D71, D81, D80 & D82 Directory adapters

- Error checking of hard disks and T64, ZipCode, G64, F64 and CRT files

- ROM manipulation (splitting, resizing, conversion to EPROM burner formats)

- And much more

What are the plans for an upcoming release?

- DFI image support (if required)

- Many FORMAT updates (released separately)

- Disassembler improvements

- Eliminate all reported errors

- Other things on my TODO list, as time allows

64COPY is Donateware: If you wish to support the continued development of 64Copy by registering or simply donating, click on the DONATE button on the webpage to send money via PayPal or see the FAQ page for how to send something.

Download: https://ist.uwaterloo.ca/~schepers/personal.html

3.7 Cracked games

Some self-installed games come up with a hacker screen but there is no indication which key or button to press.

Most of the time, you can continue by pressing a fire button either on port one or two, or the space key.

On the THEC64 Joystick it's most likely the L1, the triangle button over the left fire button.

3.8 Fastloaders

See also: 4.5 Floppy-disk drives & printer

Yes, Fastloaders are working, also when loading games via an USB stick because the Mini uses a floppy emulation.

You will find a good comparison page for Fastloaders if you follow this WiKi-link (German): https://www.c64-wiki.de/wiki/Schnelllader#Geschwin digkeitstest_Software-Schnelllader

here: https://en.wikipedia.org/wiki/Fast_loader

and here (German): https://www.mingos-commodorepage.com/tutori-als/c64fastloader.php?title=Spiele%20schneller%20laden%20mit%20 Fastloader

3.8.1 Fastloaders in commercial games

This page shows an overview of commercial games that use an built-in Fastloader: https://www.luigidifraia.com/c64/docs/tapeloaders.html

3.9 Operating systems

See also: 5.6 Mouse, 4.6 80 columns

There are two groups of operating systems for the C64, one of these is meant to be as compatible as possible. The differences are simply, changed floppy routines to improve loading times and better operation through additional commands or by presetting the function keys. In order to be able to use these operating systems, the original Kernal ROM was usually exchanged for a changed ROM. Often, switch boards were also installed in the C64 to be able to switch quickly between the operating systems.

The second group of operating systems has broken new ground. You can find UNIX derivatives as well as graphical operating systems. Some of them offer completely new functions such as an IP stack. However, this type of operating system is no longer compatible with the existing software. Due to their size, these operating systems usually can no longer be accommodated in a ROM, but are loaded from a diskette. This way, of course, valuable main memory is lost and to start takes a correspondingly long time. Nevertheless, I would like to introduce this very kind of operating system, which offers completely new possibilities to the C64 user, here!

GEOS (Graphic Environment Operating System) - Berkely Softworks GEOS is probably one of the best-known alternative operating systems for the C64, the first real and for the longest time, the only graphical operating system for the C64. It was released in 1986 in version 1.2. There was also a Spanish version 1.2, which was added to the Argentinean Drean C64C under the name Drean GEOS. Version 1.3 was finally released in German and in version 1.5 it was also included in the German C64C.

GEOS was revolutionary! Not only did you get an easy-to-use graphical user interface, there were also applications like GeoWrite and GeoPaint. To copy & paste graphics and text was possible between the different applications and control with drag-n-drop has never been easier. Not only that, the GEOS been further developed to version 2.0. A whole range of useful add-on programs and even a GEOS-BASIC to easily program your own applications by yourself were quickly available.

The German distributor Markt+Technik http://www.mut.de/ released a version 2.5 with TopDesk and several commercial add-on programs. Especially for owners of CMD hardware like SuperCPU and hard disk there were two very interesting updates for GEOS 2.0. In 1998, Maurice Randall released an upgrade called Wheels and in 1999 MegaCom released an upgrade called MP3 (MegaPatch3).

CP/M (Control Program for Microprocessors) - CP/M was a very popular operating system at that time and was one of the few cross-platform systems alongside UNIX for mainframes. At least in America, the C64 was even advertised for CP/M. This statement was somewhat exaggerated, since it belongs to one of the most complex operating systems for the C64. Aside from the software, you needed an extra CP/M expansion card with Z80 CPU. An emulation would simply not have been possible with the computing power of a C64. Despite the relatively high effort, CP/M was not really usable for the C64. The hope to be able to use the very extensive software that existed for CP/M at that time was nipped in the bud. In contrast to the 1571 of the Commodore C128, the 1541 was not able to read CP/M disks. So, you had to wait for the software to be sold in 1541 format.

Contiki - Who says you can't surf the Internet with a Commodore C64? Programmed by Adam Dunkels, contiki http://www.sics.se/contiki/ is an open source multitasking operating system designed for microcomputers such as old home computers or embedded systems. There are ports for many of the old computers but the version for the C64 is something special. There are drivers for the C64 network cards ETH64, TFE and RRnet. With its full uIP TCP/IP stack, Contiki makes the C64 a real Internet computer.

The C64 version of Contiki has a graphical user interface with windowing, a 40- and 80-character mode, joystick control (has been dropped in version

1.2 for space reasons) and even a screen saver. To use the network capabilities, there are various applications such as a web browser, web server, telnet client, telnet server, IRC client and so on. Unfortunately, the FTP client
is still faulty. Contiki has been available for some time in version 2.x, but
the last executable port for the C64 is still version 1.2-devel1. Ready-made
floppy images can be downloaded from the CSDB homepage: http://non-
ame.c64.org/csdb/search/?content=all&search=contiki

To be able to use Contiki's network capabilities on the Internet, the C64
should be connected to a router with its network card. You still have to
configure the network manually because the DHCP client does not work
without errors either. The MAC address of the RRnet network card is set to
64-64-64-4-00-00-00 by Contiki. You should enable this MAC address on
your router if you are using a MAC filter.

GeckOS/A65 Operating System - The open source operating system
GeckOS http://www.6502.org/users/andre/osa/index.html for 6502-based
systems from André Fachat is multitasking and multithreaded capable.
Since GeckOS uses the standard library lib6502 http://www.6502.org/us-
ers/andre/osa/lib6502.html just like LUnix, both systems should be source
code compatible.

GeckOS does not have its own network card drivers, but this system is net-
work-compatible via the slip daemon. A web server is already integrated in
the slip daemon.

Unfortunately, this operating system has not been further developed for a
long time. I am also unaware of any applications that have been additionally programmed for this system. I would like to mention that this could
also be due to the fact that I have never really worked with this operating
system.

LUnix (aka LNG) - Are there still computers today for which there is no
UNIX/Linux operating system? LUnix is the LittleUNIX for the C64: http://
lng.sourceforge.net/

Operating   systems   (German):   https://www.c64-wiki.de/wiki/
Betriebssystem

3.9.1 GEOS C64

Here's the Wiki Entry (German): https://www.c64-wiki.de/wiki/GEOS

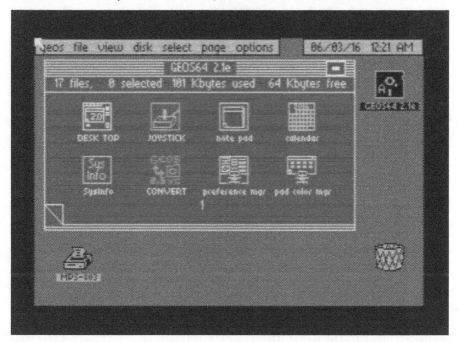

This new version of GEOS Kernal 2.1e is bootable from EPROM.

3.9.2 Contiki

Contiki is open source for the "Internet of Things". It connects microcontrollers to the Internet.

Contiki was developed in 2002 by Adam Dunkels. He named it after Thor Heyerdahl's boat Kon-Tiki.

Since version 2, the C64 is fully supported and since 2.5 also the Apple IIe. Since version 3 the processors MOS 6502/6510.

Contiki supports multitasking and networks via TCP/IP, with only 10KByte RAM and 30KByte ROM. The graphical desktop interface requires about 30KBytes RAM.

Read more on the WiKi website (German): https://www.c64-wiki.de/wiki/Contiki

3.9.3 CP/M

CP/M was developed in 1976 by Gary Kildall. The abbreviation stands for **C**ontrol **P**rogram for **M**icrocomputers. It is designed to support 8-bit processors from Intel 8080 and 8085 and the Zilog Z80.

More to read is on the Wiki website (German): https://www.c64-wiki.de/wiki/CP/M

3.9.4 LUnix

LUnix, short for "little Unix" was developed in 1993 and released in 1994. In 1997, LUnix0.1 was rewritten from scratch, the result is LNG. So LUnix and LNG were used as synonyms.

Both are free operating systems for the Commodore 64 and are distributed under the GNU General Public License (GPL) as free software.

Here's a link to LUnix Utility & Application Support: http://cbm.ficicilar.name.tr/uncorrected/lunix/lunif.html

Autoboot Disk Maker for Lunix-V0.1p4

The 'Autolunix' program is a BASIC v2.0 program which makes the disk of LUnix OS bootable.

More to read is on the webpage: http://cbm.ficicilar.name.tr/sayfa/autolunix.html

3.9.5 GOS 95 C64 operating system

GOS is an Operating System/BASIC Extension hybrid written for Commodore 64 computers between 1992 and 1995.

GOS features a disk cache, read ahead disk buffer, memory manager, memory compression, mouse support, BASIC variable transfer, linking BASIC files and external commands loaded from diskette.

Thanks to its disk cache and track buffer, the external commands are as fast as the internal commands.

Approximately 19 years later, I've recovered my GOS diskettes, work diskettes and some of the documentation and transferred them to the modern medium. However, the organization of the material and remembering/

reverse-engineering my own code takes time. I'll fill the missing information in time.

As a sample, here is a working diskette of GOS: http://cbm.ficicilar.name.tr/dosya/gos95.zip

Version: 1995.10.14-19:37

Date: October 1995

Programmer: Ilker Ficicilar

More to read is on this webpage: http://cbm.ficicilar.name.tr/commodore/gos-95-c64-operating-system-commands-part-1

3.9.6 ACE

ACE is an alternative uni-tasking operating system for the C128 and C64 that provides a Unix-like command shell. It is still in the development stage, but enough of it is complete to be useful. "ACE" means "Advanced Computing Environment" (well, advanced for the 128/64). ACE will make use of a number of hardware extensions, including REUs up to 16 Megs, RAMLinks up to 16 Megs and CMD disk drives. In addition, ACE provides custom device drivers for the screen and keyboard and a high-speed RAM disk.

ACE also includes a number of application/utility programs, including the following: a minimal ZED text editor, VT-100 terminal emulator for the SwiftLink-232 cartridge, a custom file upload/download protocol, sophisticated one-pass assembler, uuencode/uudecode, bcode/unbcode (better-than uucode), VBM bitmap viewer, file copier, crc32 error checkers, grep, tr, word count, sort, line wrapper, "more" program and a few other file utilities. Browse through the documentation for more information.

Here http://csbruce.com/cbm/ace/ you will find the downloadable and complete documentation.

3.10 Programming languages

For the C64 there are not only some functions have been added to BASIC, but also a few other programming languages have been implemented for it.

3.10.1 THEC64 Mini BASIC

This is the official guide from Retro Games on how to use BASIC: https://thec64.com/basic/

One of the titles on the GAMES CAROUSEL isn't a game at all, but gives you access to the BASIC programming language.

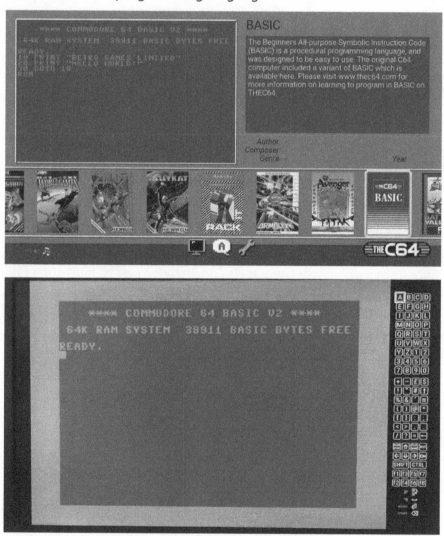

If you want to follow through the BASIC examples, we strongly recommend connecting an USB keyboard to the Mini, rather than trying to use the Virtual keyboard. Please read **CHAPTER 5: KEYBOARDS** in the User Guide PDF before starting this introduction to BASIC.

If a compatible USB memory stick (formatted to FAT32) is attached to the Mini before BASIC is launched, then you can save your BASIC code to the memory stick. See **Saving and Loading** below for further information.

If you prefer, a video of this introduction to C64 BASIC is also available.

WHAT IS BASIC?

When you turn on a C64 computer, the first thing you see is BASIC. We provide access to BASIC on the Mini for those who wish to experience programming using version 2 of the C64 variant of the **B**eginners **A**ll-purpose **S**ymbolic **I**nstruction **C**ode.

BASIC is a high-level programming language, designed to be easy to use. It is an interpreted language, meaning any BASIC instructions you type have to be translated by the computer before it can run them. This actually happens quite quickly and is done automatically by the computer.

Computers like the original C64 and the Mini natively 'talk' in machine code, which is a series of zeros (0) and ones (1). When they use machine code they operate very fast. However, people don't directly program in machine code. So, we use a different way to send instructions to the computer, using programming languages that are closer to what we are used to.

Some programming languages are a few steps closer to machine code and so they are interpreted (or translated if you prefer) quicker than those that aren't.

BASIC has always been an excellent introduction to programming for complete beginners even though it is quite a few steps away from machine code.

Learning to program using C64 BASIC teaches you the mindset of programming and it also teaches you how to type on a keyboard. Both of these skills are important to learn.

BASIC KEYWORDS

C64 BASIC has a series of keywords that tell the computer what to do next. Learn those and you will be writing BASIC code in no time. There are 71 BASIC keywords to discover.

If you think 71 sounds a lot, don't worry. You don't have to learn them all at once. Many of them are related to doing mathematical calculations and only come into play when you start doing more complex coding. More on keywords later!

LAUNCHING C64 BASIC

When you first launch BASIC from the GAMES CAROUSEL on the HOME screen, you see a blue screen. It begins by showing how much computer memory is available for programming. Underneath that information is a READY prompt and underneath that is a steadily blinking square cursor.

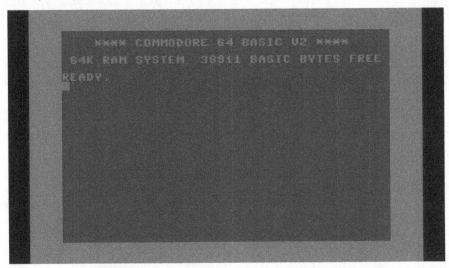

Staring at the cursor won't get you very far. It's ready and waiting for you to enter your first BASIC commands.

There are two ways of entering BASIC code. You can type it in and press RETURN. The computer will immediately try and run your code. However, to repeat the same code later on, you have to type it in again. That doesn't sound so good. The second method is a lot more efficient. You place numbers at the start of each line of your code that tells the computer in which order to run them. The great thing is that using line numbers also means it won't run your code until you type the RUN keyword *and* it means you don't have to type it all in again (as long as you don't turn off the computer).

YOUR FIRST BASIC PROGRAM

Below is an example of BASIC program. We will look at each line of code in turn before doing this on the Mini.

There are three separate lines of BASIC code to explain.

```
10 PRINT "RETRO GAMES LIMITED"
20 PRINT "HELLO WORLD!"
30 GOTO 10
```

Line 10 uses the keyword PRINT which sends whatever appears between the quotation marks "" to the computer screen (and not to a printer as you might expect!).

Line 20 does the same as line 10 but will send different words to the screen.

Line 30 instructs the computer to go to line 10, which puts the computer in a loop of running line 10, then line 20, then line 30 telling it to go back to line 10 again and so on.

The line numbers are in units of ten just in case we want to insert extra lines of code, e.g. a line 15 that comes between line 10 and line 20. If you type a line of code that begins with the same line number as an existing line, the new line will replace the old one as soon as you press RETURN, without any warnings. If you type just the line number and nothing else then press RETURN, you delete that line number.

Now type each line exactly as you see it above. Press RETURN at the end of each numbered line to commit that line to the computer's memory and to move down a line, before starting to type the next one.

Press RETURN at the end of line 30.

If you make a mistake, use the Backspace key on your USB keyboard (or press the C button on the joystick when using the Virtual keyboard). Each time you press will erase the character immediately to the left of the cursor's position on the screen.

If you're happy that you've typed everything in correctly, type the RUN keyword (without a line number). Your code will then run!

If you're wondering how to stop your new BASIC code from running forever, try pressing ESC (on an USB keyboard) or RUN/STOP (if using the virtual keyboard). You have instructed the Mini to BREAK into your code. Don't worry – it's not as bad as it sounds!

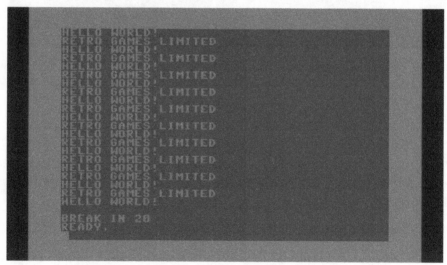

To see that your code is still intact, you can type the following keyword at the square cursor:

```
LIST
```

Your three lines of code are displayed, safe and sound just as they were the last time you saw them.

BASIC Keywords

Believe it or not, you've already used four BASIC keywords. To prove it, here is a table showing all 71 of them.

```
ABS      AND    ASC    ATN     CHR$   CLOSE  CLR      CMD
CONT     COS    DATA   DEF     DIM    END    EXP      FN
FOR      FRE    GET    GET$    GOSUB  GOTO   IF       INPUT
INPUT$   INT    LEFT$  LEN     LET    LIST   LOAD     LOG
MID$     NEW    NEXT   NOT     ON     OPEN   OR       PEEK
POKE     POS    PRINT  PRINT$  READ   REM    RESTORE  RETURN
RIGHT$   RND    RUN    SAVE    SGN    SIN    SPC      SQR
STATUS   STEP   STOP   STR$    SYS    TAB    TAN      THEN
TIME     TIME$  TO     USR     VAL    VERIFY WAIT
```

We're now going to slightly change your code so that it only prints the two lines of text five times before stopping, rather than going on forever.

```
5 FOR A=1 TO 5
10 PRINT "RETRO GAMES LIMITED"
20 PRINT "HELLO WORLD!"
30 NEXT A
```

You should immediately notice that we have added a line number 5 and we have changed what was on line 30.

Look at these two new lines of code for a moment and ignore lines 10 and 20 in-between. These lines introduce two new concepts to your BASIC knowledge as well as two new keywords.

One concept is defining and using variables in your code. In this example, we are using 'A' as a container to temporarily store a number inside. The letter A was chosen but it could easily have been the word 'WORLD', in this case it could have read…

```
5 FOR WORLD=1 TO 5
```

(lines 10 and 20 remain the same as before)

```
30 NEXT WORLD
```

… and your program would still have worked. You could also have changed the number at the end of your line of code from 5 to 6. Variable names are chosen by you and can (almost) be anything you like. However, there are rules to naming these handy variables for storing things in.

You can't use reserved keywords used by BASIC or by the C64 for its own system variables. How do you know which ones can't be used? Well, if you had used LIST as your variable name, running the program would have produced:

```
?SYNTAX ERROR IN 5
```

It's not the most helpful of errors, but if the Mini returns that error, you know something is wrong. Remember the list of C64 BASIC keywords? Don't use any of those as names for your variables and you can't go far wrong.

Try to keep your variable names short, but relevant where you can. If your code isn't overly complex, then you can just use A, B, C and so on, just as long as you remember what they are used for!

Types of Variable

The only other thing to know is that there are three types of variable and they are defined by what type of information is stored in them.

The two most common that you will use are **integer** and **string** variables.

An integer is simply a whole number, so no fractions or decimal points. A string is letters or letters and numbers.

How do you know which type of variable you want to use? For integers, you just use a name for your variable, without anything else, e.g. WORLD. For strings, you add a $ to the end of the variable name, so RECIPE$ might be used to store the name of your favourite cake or biscuit recipe, e.g. "Rocky Road".

So, looking at your amended BASIC example, we know that 'A' is used to store a whole number (which can actually be between -32768 up to 32767). In our example, it is only going to reach a maximum value of 5.

Now let's discuss the FOR and NEXT keywords. These are paired together and create a FOR... NEXT loop. What this does is from the FOR keyword, the computer stores a number inside 'A' that starts at 1 and will end at 5 (in this particular example).

Each time the running code encounters the NEXT 'variable' (NEXT A in our example), it returns to the line with the FOR keyword and by increments (adds one to) the current number stored in the variable called 'A'. The code then runs each line of code it comes across afterwards (i.e. line 10 and line 20) until it hits NEXT A again, then it returns to the FOR keyword and repeats the process until the value of 'A' equals 5, then it stops.

So, add in line 5 exactly as shown previously, change line 30 and then RUN the amended code and see what happens.

Now, it would be useful to show what the current value of 'A' is. Add a new line 25:

```
25 PRINT A
```

Now RUN your code again.

You can now see the two lines of printed text are followed by a number that goes up by one each time, e.g. 1, 2, 3, 4, 5.

It's useful to see the value stored in variable 'A' as you can now see how it changes within that FOR… NEXT loop, adding one automatically whenever it reaches NEXT.

Let's now make this look a little better by adding something to line 25.

```
25 PRINT "VARIABLE 'A' IS NOW";A
```

The semi-colon at the end tells BASIC to keep the cursor on the same line as the text it is printing to the screen and then display the value of the variable A.

RUN this latest version of your code.

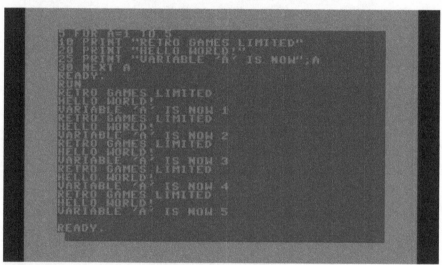

That's a little better. It is now clear what those numbers mean and we've learned how to place the value of a variable into a PRINT command at the same time!

That almost concludes the introduction to C64 BASIC. However, before we finish, let's learn how you can keep (save) your code so it can you can run it again and amend it in future.

SAVING AND LOADING

On the Mini, you have two available methods for saving your BASIC programs:

1.   Press the MENU button and select 'Save/Load game' and then save to an available slot on the Mini as you would do for a game. See **CHAPTER 4: PLAYING GAMES** in the User Guide PDF for more details on saving and loading to slots.

2.   If a compatible USB memory stick (formatted to FAT32) is attached to the Mini *before* BASIC is launched, then you can save your BASIC code to the memory stick. When launching BASIC, the Mini looks for a specific disk image file on the memory stick. If the file isn't found, then a *THEC64-drive8.d64* file is automatically created on the USB memory stick for you. You will then be able to save and load to and from this file from BASIC.

Please note that to accommodate THEC64 Joystick, an USB Keyboard and an USB memory stick at the same time, you need to connect a separate USB hub (not supplied) which gives access to additional USB ports. Retro Games Ltd cannot guarantee that all USB hubs will work with the Mini and some hubs require a separate power source.

SAVE

With a compatible USB memory stick connected, you can save to the disk image using the standard SAVE to disk command, e.g.

```
SAVE "RGL",8
```

The name of the file goes between the speech marks and it can be whatever you like, as long as it isn't longer than 15 characters. In this example, it's nice and short. The number 8 after the filename is a device ID number that is allocated to the disk image file on your USB memory stick.

Press RETURN afterwards to begin the save.

BASIC will report 'SAVING' followed by your chosen filename and when it is completed, it returns to the READY prompt and the square cursor.

Be aware that if you use a filename that has been previously saved to the same disk, your new file will overwrite the old file without any warning.

VERIFY

You can check that the save worked by using the VERIFY keyword.

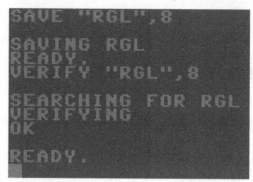

```
VERIFY "RGL",8
```

If everything is okay, you will see VERIFYING followed by OK.

LOAD

Once more, ensure that the same USB storage device is connected to the Mini before you run BASIC and then type the following command in BASIC to get your program back.

```
LOAD "RGL",8
```

What's on my disk?

From BASIC, you can look at a disk and see what files are in it. To do that requires use of the LOAD command, but in a slightly different way from before. Instead of typing a filename, we are using the reserved variable $.

```
LOAD "$",8
```

BASIC will report SEARCHING FOR $ followed by LOADING and then it returns to the READY prompt once again.

To see what's on the disk is simple. Just type the following command:

```
LIST
```

Instead of listing BASIC code, this time the command shows what is on the disk.

```
READY.
LOAD "$",8

SEARCHING FOR $
LOADING
READY.
LIST

0  "THEC64                       "  01  2A
1     "RGL"                              PRG
663 BLOCKS FREE.
READY.
```

In the above example, we have just one program on the disk and it's the program we just saved called RGL. The program uses up 1 block on the disk and there are 663 blocks still available to save programs on in the future.

Be aware that if you load the directory of a disk and have some BASIC code on the C64 at the same time, the $ listing will replace the BASIC listing in the computer's memory and you will lose your program (if you haven't already saved it).

If you want to use multiple disks, then you will need to use a different USB memory stick for each disk, or temporarily rename the files because the .D64 file is always saved with the same filename – THEC64-drive8.d64 – each time.

Read Only

If you don't have an USB storage device attached, but decide to try saving to device 8 anyway, BASIC will look like it has successfully saved but when you load the directory of the disk it will be empty. This is because without USB storage, BASIC uses a disk image that can only be read, not saved to. The tell-tale sign is the name of the disk which is read-only. The disk is completely empty and cannot have anything saved to it.

To overcome this, you can always save in one of the four save slots, switch off the Mini, insert an USB memory stick into a spare USB port, switch the Mini back on, load BASIC, restore the save slot and then save to the D64 disk image using the SAVE command detailed earlier. Device 8 will now be the disk image on your USB memory stick.

LEARN MORE

Before we finish, how many C64 BASIC commands have you used now?

```
ABS      AND     ASC    ATN    CHR$   CLOSE  CLR      CMD
CONT     COS     DATA   DEF    DIM    END    EXP      FN
FOR      FRE     GET    GET$   GOSUB  GOTO   IF       INPUT
INPUT$   INT     LEFT$  LEN    LET    LIST   LOAD     LOG
MID$     NEW     NEXT   NOT    ON     OPEN   OR       PEEK
POKE     POS     PRINT  PRINT$ READ   REM    RESTORE  RETURN
RIGHT$   RND     RUN    SAVE   SGN    SIN    SPC      SQR
STATUS   STEP    STOP   STR$   SYS    TAB    TAN      THEN
TIME     TIME$   TO     USR    VAL    VERIFY WAIT
```

You're up to 11/71 commands already! We hope this small introduction has given you an interest to learn more. There are plenty of online resources available. Also, have a look at our Links page: https://thec64.com/links/

3.10.2 BASICs and extensions

These are all the BASIC variations I have found:

GERMANBASIC (64'er BASIC in German)

SIMONS BASIC (Extended)

ULTRA BASIC (Extended)

WARSAW BASIC (Extended)

DRAGO BASIC (Extended)

SUPER BASIC (Extended)

GRAPHIC BASIC (Extended for Graphics)

SPEECH BASIC V2.7

BASIC 4.0

This extension for BASIC could be loaded into two different RAM areas. Included in the archive are two reference books.

If you know some more, please let me know - and where to get them. Thank you.

3.10.2.1 Tips for faster BASIC

This webpage offers a lot of tips to be faster with BASIC. The page is written in Turkish but is very readable with e.g. the online Google Translator.

Here: http://cbm.ficicilar.name.tr/sayfa/c64-Tuna_Ertemalp-Hizli_Basic.html

3.10.3 BASIC compilers

A BASIC compiler converts your BASIC programs into the machine language for speed boosts of up to 40x.

3.10.3.1 BASIC Compiler

This version has demo programs included on the disk converted to English by Juan (Thank you). Also included is the Manual as PDF.

BASIC-Boss v2.42 was released in 1989 by Thilo Herrmann.

3.10.3.2 BASIC 64 Compiler v1.03

This program also converts programs written in BASIC into machine language for a huge performance gain.

3.10.4 Other languages

This is an overview of other languages than BASIC that are available for the C64:

• G-PASCAL V3.0

• OXFORD PASCAL V2.1

• EightBall - Download: https://github.com/bobbimanners/EightBall
  EightBall is an interpreter and bytecode compiler for a novel structured programming language. It runs on a number of 6502-based vintage systems (C64, VIC20, Apple //e) and may also be compiled as a 32 bit Linux executable. The system also includes a simple line editor and the EightBall Virtual Machine, which runs the bytecode generated by the compiler.

• Read more: http://everythingc64.proboards.com/search/results?captcha_id=captcha_search&what_at_least_

one=c64+mini&who_only_made_by=0&display_as=0&search=Search
#ixzz5JAWz7Zl4

There is a pre-built disk-image for C64 and VIC20 and also full documentation for the project.

This is a free software project. Full source is available on GitHub.

Current version is v0.55. This project is still a work-in-progress.

To download the image you have to be registered at GitHub (Free Account).

- MSE (Machine code Editor)

    If you want to learn to code/program in assembly, have a look here: http://tnd64.unikat.sk/assemble_it.html. It's a free tutorial for easy learning. Additionally, you will get the fitting tools for free: http://tnd64.unikat.sk/ass_example_pics/TND_User_Tooldisk.zip

If you know some more, please let me know - and where to get them. Thank you.

3.10.5 CBM.prg Studio

CBM prg Studio (http://www.ajordison.co.uk/) is a Windows Integrated Development Environment (IDE) which allows you to type a BASIC or machine code program and convert it to a '.prg' file (as used by the Mini, an original C64 and a number of other programs). It also includes character, sprite and screen editors and a fully featured 6510/65816 debugger.

3.10.6 C64 Bites

This is the easiest way to start programming Commodore 64. Life is too short to read twenty-year-old books. Learn BASIC and 6502 Assembly with bite-sized video tutorials today! https://64bites.com/

3.11 64 Doctor

See also: 5.2 Joysticks, 5.3 Keyboard

64 Doctor is a complete system tester for the C64. Devices tested are: RAM, keyboard, video, audio, joysticks, disk-drive, printer and cassette.

In order to test all, you need a hardware harness. But this only works on an original C64.

3.12 Viruses

Don't panic!

The only "viruses" for the C64 would render the BAM, the directory of a floppy disk, unusable. However, since there is no floppy in the real sense of the word, this virus cannot become active either.

3.13 Emulators

3.13.1 PET Emulator

The PET Emulator by Bob Fairbairn reconfigures a Commodore 64 to emulate a 40-column PET Computer (model 1977–1979).

3.13.2 ZX Spectrum emulator

The "Spectrum Simulator" is an emulator that enables the BASIC of the ZX Spectrum on the C64. The program was published in 1985 by Whitby Computers.

It was written to illustrate how powerful the C64 was in its day.

3.13.3 MS-DOS simulator

This MS-DOS simulator from 1986 for the C64 is essentially a command line interpreter of MS-DOS Version 1.x/2.0. It was published in the Commodore Computer Club Diskmag by "Publishers Systems Editoriale". At the end of 1987, the second version of the simulator was released which was already more mature.

Via this link you can learn more about it: https://www.c64-wiki.de/wiki/MS-DOS_Simulator

3.13.4 GW-BASIC

GW-BASIC has been a popular Microsoft programming language for PC, Atari and other computers since 1981 in the 1980s.

This emulation was very well implemented.

Read more about it here: https://www.c64-wiki.de/wiki/GW-BASIC_Emulator

4 The hardware

To answer a frequently asked question, the Mini is not based on a Raspberry PI and also not on Android.

Question: Will the hardware change in future versions?

Answer: Retro Games may upgrade the memory or SoC and supporting hardware to take advantage of better cost options.

Question: Will there be support of an onboard Micro-SD? The Slot place is reserved on the board for this purpose?

Answer: The SD card footprint on the PCB is a remnant of the prototype PCB. It is not functional and will be removed in later iterations.

Question: Do you plan to use serial numbers on the case and if not, why haven't you used them by now as seen on the original C64? This is important for collectors.

Answer: Retro Games has no current plan to do this on the standard retail Mini, but they are continually reviewing all options and possibly might happen for future versions or potential special edition versions.

Question: Will there be a gold edition if you produce 100,000 or 500,000 or 1 million Minis?

Answer: Retro Games is looking at many potential special editions if demand is shown by the public.

4.1 Facts and figures

Here are the hardware facts:

- CPU: ALLWINNER A20 ARM Cortex-A7 Dual-Core clocked with 1GHZ

- GPU: Mali400 MP2 clocked with 300MHz Dual Core

- 256MB SDRAM

- 128MB NAND Flash Storage

- Status LED (Power On)

- Recovery button (function unknown)

- UBoot-button - U-Boot is a bootstrap software that runs on different processors, especially on microcontrollers. It is mainly used in the field of embedded systems.

- 2 USB 2.0 ports

- 105mm x 205mm x 35mm

- Video and audio via HDMI

- OS: Linux derivative

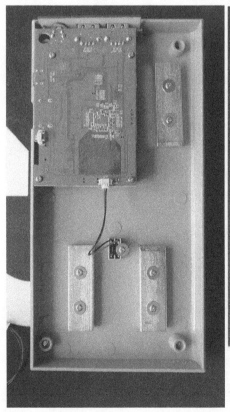

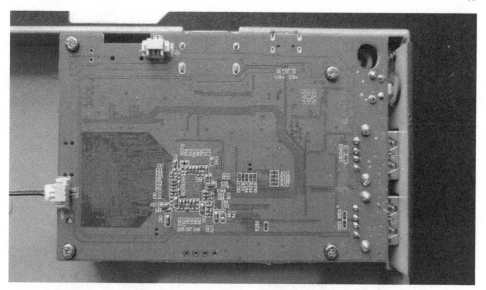

FEATURES

- Accurate C64 operation

- NTSC & PAL Display modes (60 & 50 Hz) 720p

- Pixel filter options (sharp, CRT, scanline emulation)

- Pixel perfect graphics

- Save game function

- 2 USB 2.0 ports

- Supports firmware upgrades via USB flash drive (Note: keys are non-functional)

WHAT'S IN THE BOX?

- THEC64 MINI console with 64 pre-installed games

- Classic USB Joystick

- HDMI cable

- USB cable for power supply which is not included

- * AC USB adaptor not included

4.1.1 64 Games

At firmware 1.0.8:

Alleykat, Anarchy, The Arc of Yesod, Armalyte, Avenger, Battle Valley, Bounder, California Games, Chip's Challenge, Confuzion, Cosmic Causeway, Creatures, Cyberdyne Warrior, Cybernoid, Cybernoid II, Deflektor, Everyone's a Wally, Firelord, Gribbly's Day Out, Hawkeye, Heartland, Herobotix, Highway Encounter, Hunter's Moon, Hysteria, Impossible Mission, Impossible Mission II, Insects in Space, Mega-Apocalypse, Mission A.D., Monty Mole, Monty on the Run, Nebulus, Netherworld, Nobby the Aardvark, Nodes of Yesod, Paradroid, Pitstop II, Ranarama, Robin of the Wood, Rubicon, Skate Crazy, Skool Daze, Slayer, Snare, Speedball, Speedball 2, Spin Dizzy, Star Paws, Steel, Stormlord, Street Sports Baseball, Summer Games II, Super Cycle, Temple of Apshai Trilogy, Thing on a Spring, Thing Bounces Back, Trailblazer, Uchi Mata, Uridium, Who Dares Wins II, Winter Games, World Games, Zynaps

4.2 The joystick

See also: 5.2 Joysticks

The Mini joystick is very different from the most similar looking, Competition Pro.

The difference is huge. The plastic seems not to be ABS plastic and is relatively weaker. There is a thick metal shaft running through the old Competition Pro and nothing but plastic on the THEC64 Mini one. The fire buttons are not as arcade-like and has a loose feel and perform not very accurately. There isn't much physical feedback compared to the 80's joystick either.

It functions great with a smooth confirmed 'click' and a huge rubber ring keeping the stick free from making creaking noises even if there is a weak spring instead of the rubber ring on the new one.

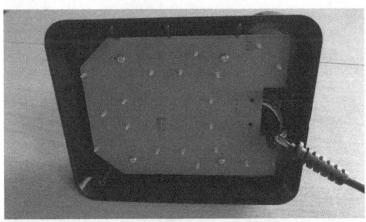

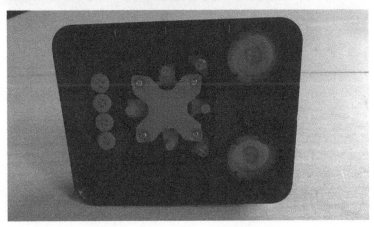

The reason why the Mini has weights on the inside at its bottom is the same reason that there are some in the joystick as well. This way, it lays more full weight on the hand.

It's amazing how they look the same but are so different.

I guess this was done due to the production costs.

Pinout:

Here is the pinout for the chip on the joystick board:

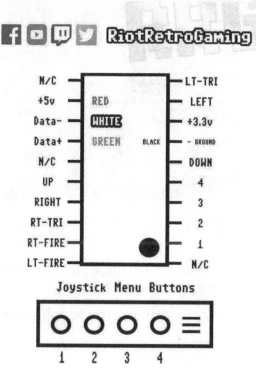

Auto-Fire:

With the pinout, you have the information where you can find the pins for extra connection on an auto fire electronic. These little circuits are easy to assemble and to find by google search "LM555CN auto fire joystick"

Arcade Buttons:

The joystick has very few free spaces where the simple Arcade buttons (Fire) are to exchange them with real Arcade buttons with micro switches. Maybe you will give it a try anyway?

This google link will show you what to search for: "joystick arcade button red micro switch"

The advantage would be to have the original THEC64 Mini joystick with its extra features and some decent fire buttons.

Please remember – any alterations you are doing are at your own risk and responsibility!

4.2.1 Virtual Joystick

For firmware v1.2.0 and above

Connecting a USB keyboard (that includes a numeric keypad and function keys up to at least F11) to THEC64 Mini gives access to a Virtual Joystick as well as all the benefits of a real keyboard.

Use the Virtual Joystick to navigate menus, select options and play games without needing a USB Joystick, or use the Virtual Joystick as a second controller if you only have one USB joystick attached.

You can choose between two Virtual Joystick layouts. Both layouts use the numeric keypad and the function keys F9, F10 and F11.

The current layout depends on whether your keyboard's 'Num Lock' key is in the ON or OFF state. By default, the 'Num Lock' is OFF when you connect a USB keyboard to THEC64 Mini. Press the 'Num Lock' key to change from OFF to ON or vice versa. Some USB keyboards include a 'Num Lock' LED to show its current state.

Num Lock OFF (default)Num Lock ON

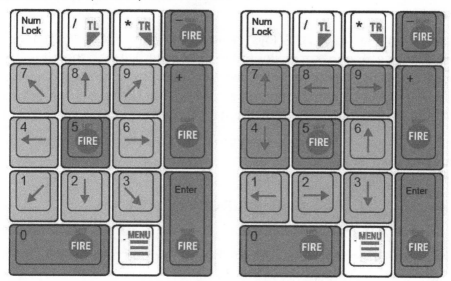

Diagonals are achieved by pressing UP+RIGHT, UP+LEFT, DOWN+LEFT or DOWN+RIGHT together

Note that the 'Num Lock' ON layout gives you more choice. You can mix and match the LEFT, RIGHT, UP and DOWN keys if you want to. For example, using 6, 3, 8 and 9 instead of 1, 2, 6 and 3.

Regardless of which layout you use, you have a choice of which keys to use as Left and Right FIRE, as you can see from the diagram above. The . key (the , key on a German USB keyboard) always acts as the Joystick's MENU button, giving access to the usual Save/load game, Virtual keyboard and Exit game options. The TL and TR buttons are / and * respectively.

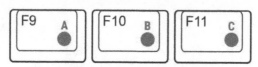

Keys F9, F10 and F11 perform the same functions as THEC64 Joystick buttons A, B and C.

Allocating Controllers

When you run a C64 program from the GAMES CAROUSEL or via the File Loader, THEC64 Mini will always allocate the primary controller to the joystick that selected the program, whether that is a USB joystick or the Virtual Joystick.

If there is an unallocated USB joystick attached, then THEC64 Mini chooses that as the secondary controller (if one is required). If not, then it will allocate the Virtual Joystick as the secondary controller, assuming that a suitable USB keyboard is attached and assuming that the Virtual Joystick has not already been allocated as the primary controller.

THEC64 Mini can only allocate one Virtual Joystick, even if you were to connect two USB keyboards.

4.3 Pin assignment & buttons

See also: 7.1.1 UART Interface Root access, 7.1.2.1 FEL Mode

If you like to experience this with the board, it's good to know which pins are available and what purpose they have.

Here is what is known so far and have been confirmed:

From the left to right: 3.3V, RxD, TxD, GND (solder point on the right)

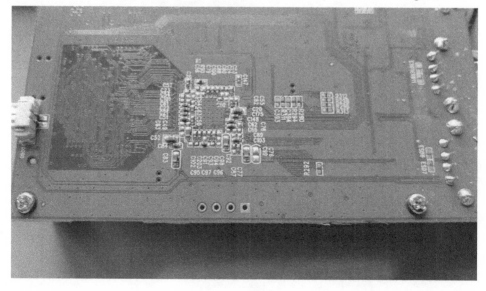

Retro Games: The button heading to the bottom of the Mini was just to make set up at the factory easier for the workers. For actual use it is no longer needed hence why the sticker then covers it. It's not important to users.

There is much more information to find at Forum64 https://www. forum64.de/index.php?thread/81623-thec64-mini-modding-uart-schnittstelle-f%C3%BCr-seriellen-root-zugriff/&postID=1257891#post1257891.

4.4 Power supply

See also: 5 USB, 5.4 USB hub

Officially 1 Ampere is expected, but previous experience shows that at least 1.5A is better to supply USB hubs and keyboards (e.g. when they are illuminated) with sufficient power.

4.5 Floppy-disk drives & printer

See also: 3.6 Fastloaders

In principle, it is possible to connect a real CBM drive such as 1541/1570/1571/1581 to the Mini via an USB adapter. However, I found no way to access the drive directly from the Mini, even if the drive got the ID 9. This is because the Mini always works with 8 and so it could have created conflicts.

Nevertheless, here is a suggestion for you to experiment. If you managed it, please write me and I will show the solution in the next edition of the book.

XU1541

You can access a real Floppy-Drive with an adapter cable or similar solutions, as shown below.

Additionally, you will need a program to access the drive, like OpenCBM: http://opencbm.sourceforge.net/

There are several adapter solutions on the market which you can use. Here are some examples:

The XU1541 USB adapter is available from www.commodore16.com XU1541 was originally developed by Till Harbaum and is the modern variation of the classic X1541 cable that made it possible to connect the drive via a PC printer port many years ago. If you like to build and use the soldering iron, here at http://www.trikaliotis.net/xu1541 and here https://www.mingos-commodorepage.com/tutorials/c64xu1541.php you will find further information about the XU1541, as well as assembly instructions and the required firmware.

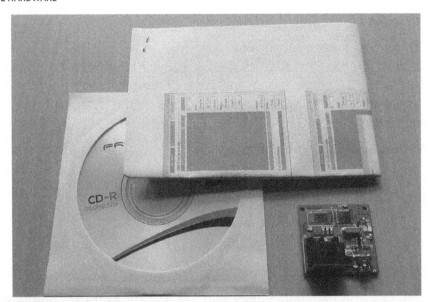

ZoomFloppy

RETRO Innovations https://www.c64-wiki.de/wiki/RETRO_Innovations builds an USB interface that enables data exchange with Commodore devices via the IEC connection (serial port) or printers with a PC. The hardware is similar to the XUM1541 and is powered via the USB port. The driver software is included in OpenCBM http://opencbm.sourceforge.net/.

Yes, **Fastloader** is supported and working.

For more information see 3.6 Fastloaders.

4.6 80 columns

See also: 3.7 Operating systems

Can the Mini display 80 columns?

In short, yes. The hardware is fast enough and the software emulations are accurate to display text sharper than on the original C64 thanks to the HDMI signal.

Tip: 53 <> 80 Columns

Alternatively, you should try this neat little program that "only" shows 53Columns but because of that, it's much more readable using more space for each character. David the 8-Bit Guy programmed it and you can download it here http://www.the8bitguy.com/download-davids-software/.

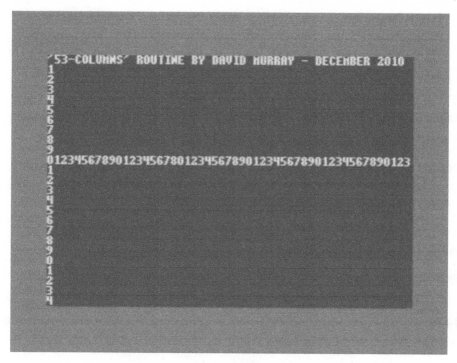

4.7 The differences between THEC64 Mini PAL and NTSC

First to mention is the other collection of games. Retro Games did this due to the fact that in the US, other games were more popular than in europe. Removed are Armalyte, Bounder, Deflektor, Hawkeye, Monty Mole, Rubicon, Star Paws, Steel, Uchi Mata and replaced with the NTSC versions Break Dance, Destroyer, Gateway to Apshai, Jumpman 2, Silicon Warrior, Street Sports - Basketball, Street Sports - Soccer, Sword of Fargol, West Bank.

Secondly some games got other names. Nebulus is Tower Toppler, Trailbalzer II is Cosmic Causeway and Thing Bounces Back is Coil Cop.

4.8 Video output

Question: The joystick reaction time is slow and the lag makes some games unplayable.
And the sound seems to be slower at different games.

Retro Games: This is a problem for two reasons. The reaction time of the joysticks are regularly fine, but because of a delay in processing the HDMI-Signal in some monitors or TVs, it just seems to be a joystick problem. In fact, the HDMI processing is slow. You can fix this and try it out with another monitor or TV.

Most TVs today are 1080p and the Mini outputs 720p so the TVs have to upscale the picture which may result in a lag.

Another possibility to solve this is to disable all HDMI-Features in your TV. Every feature like motion smoothing or noise reduction cost some processing time which will increase the delay a bit.

One other thing to try would be to change the HDMI port as on some TVs one port is specially for or just runs a little better for gaming.

Secondly, the screen mode you choose changes the delay a bit. Try around to find the best fit. The best should be the "Full screen pixel perfect" option.

There is a C64 program with which you can test the delay: http://gurce. net/c64mini_files/delaytest.d64

Or type in a Google search for "delaytest.d64".

Question: How much did they change the joystick port latency and will there be more improvements of that kind?

Retro Games: There are many things going on outside the actual emulation. For example, the GPU buffers. After there were reports of latency in some games, it was discovered that the GPU buffering could be predicted. As a result, there were some reschedules of the internal events to preempt this.

4.8.1 Display Lag database

The input delay is the time it takes for a display to process a keystroke during the game. For an excellent gaming experience, a display with high input delay must be avoided, as the gameplay feels sluggish and insensitive. The input delay database helps to avoid delay indications, as it is the world's largest database for it. We therefore recommend the devices marked Excellent or Great, as they offer the least input delay in game mode. The displays of the same model series have an almost identical input delay across all size ranges. Most displays can be ordered via a direct link on Amazon. Share it with your friends! Thank you.

Go to: https://displaylag.com/display-database/

4.9 SID in stereo
See also: 12.4 SID music, 12.4.2 Commodore SID 6581 Datasheet

So far, the sound emulation is done as a 6581, so there is no "real" stereo for the Mini. The audio output via HDMI is the mono channelled to stereo.

Retro Games experimented with stereo, but some SID effects deliberately use two channels that interfere with each other and does not work with stereo, so they left it as mono.

So far, I don't know of any hardware or software solutions to change that.

4.10 Network / LAN WiFi FTP
See also: 12.1.1 C64 web browser

Question: Is there a plan for supporting LAN, WiFi or FTP? F.e. for keyboards, joysticks and File transfer.

Retro Games: No. Retro Games made the hardware deliberately as cost-effective as possible and so does not support this. If we added WiFi, that would increase the cost and user interface complexity of the Mini unnecessarily and be used by only a small percentage of its users.

For interested parties there is a discussion with ideas at the http://thec-64community.online/thread/22/wounder-add-network-thec64-mini

By now, there is also no working way for a LAN functionality whatsoever. If you know a way, please let me know. I will include this in the next version of this book.

4.10 Expansion- user- serial-ports

Question: Is there any plan to support the user-, tape- or expansion port?

Retro Games: Electrical compatibility is not possible with emulation. However, what can or will be realized in the successor of the Mini is still open. Maybe there's a surprise awaiting here.

4.12 Memory expansion

Question: Could a REU (RAM Expansion Unit) be emulated by using internal RAM? And if so, how can it be used?

Retro Games: This is currently not supported. The idea is not new and has already been discussed, but has not yet been implemented in favor of other updates or innovations.

5 USB

See also: 4.4 Power supply, 5.2 Joysticks

5.1 USB sticks

See also: 2.1 How to upgrade

It seems that simply formatting an USB stick with FAT32 is not enough. The Mini also expects an MBR (Master Boot Record) within the first 512 bytes of the stick.

If you are curious and want to understand the details, Google search: What is an MBR?

Question: Why do I need to format or convert an USB drive for the Mini to FAT32?

Answer: The Mini operates with a system that only supports USB-Pen drives formatted with FAT32.

- NTFS reads/writes files larger than 4 GB, creates a partition larger than 32 GB, compresses files and stores space, has better memory management (less fragmentation), allows more clusters on a large drive (less wasted spaces), adds user permissions for individual files and folders and encrypts file system.

- FAT32 is compatible with almost all operating systems, takes up less space on the USB drive and has fewer disk writing operations (faster and less memory consumption).

Like other hard drives, the USB drive organizes in a cluster and the size of the allocation unit describes the size of a single cluster. Larger clusters result in more waste or empty space, while smaller clusters mean smaller pieces of a file that take longer to access and the USB drive slows down. So, if you want to store large files on your USB drive, a large cluster size will make it run faster. But if you want to save small files or run programs from your USB drive, a smaller cluster size will save space.

5.1.1 Maximum size USB drive

One of the most common questions regarding USB is what USB-stick sizes are supported?

Quite large ones have been tested, but there is no 'officially supported' maximum size currently.

5.2 Joysticks

See also: 3.9 64 Doctor, 5 USB, 4.2 The joystick

Question: Will the next joystick have micro switches and when will it be released?

Retro Games: We are discussing a 'pro' version of a joystick and may look at retail options for this.
     Hence, it will not be included in the original package.

5.2.1 Joystick compatibility

A common question to the Mini is its joystick compatibility. So which joysticks are supported?

Regularly all joysticks that have 8 buttons (see 13 FAQ) should work. But there is no guarantee for that.

Below you will find a list of officially supported joysticks.

Via the links to the Forum64, you will find compatibility tests for a lot more joysticks. Hopefully, you will find yours.

TIP: To configure as little as possible on the joystick, e.g. for extra keys that use many games, use a joystick with at least 8 buttons, e.g. a joypad.

The supplied first-generation joystick has no micro switches such as the Competition Pro.

Retro Games wants to change this and deliver a version with micro switches. At this time, they are checking out the retail market for this.

Micro switches are, so to speak, real mechanical buttons, in contrast to membrane or tactile keys.

TIP: The Mini joystick is recognized in Windows and you can use it to play games :)

Please note that the hardware results listed are based on user experiences shared via theC64 community forum (also see old forum posts) and theC64 Facebook discussion group. As such, no one can officially confirm the accuracy of all reports, so please use caution, personal research and consideration when deciding on what hardware you plan on buying. If something listed here doesn't work out the way you hoped, please share those experiences via the forums and let others learn from your experiences too. In doing so, this page can be updated over time as soon as any incorrect/inaccurate entries become aware.

Joysticks/Gamepads

Reports from users:

The Mini FAQ states that it requires a gamepad with at least 8 buttons in order to work, although there have been reports from some people of getting gamepads with fewer buttons to work.

Some people have also mentioned that you should use an USB power adapter of 2A or higher (maybe even up to 2.5A?)

Even for working controllers listed, there have been comments that some buttons haven't been mapped ideally and it would be preferable if a future firmware update permitted the user to re-map buttons to suit their controllers.

More to read is on this webpage! https://gurce.net/c64mini/hardware_compatibility_lists

Joystick Reference lists:

https://gurce.net/oldforum/229-joysticks-pads-that-work-on-the-c64-mini.txt

https://gurce.net/oldforum/161-alternative-joypad-and-new-games.txt

https://gurce.net/oldforum/122-working-non-working-USB-sticks.txt

https://gurce.net/oldforum/103-one-question-that-has-not-been-ask-can-you-use-a-USB-to-db9-adapter.txt

https://gurce.net/oldforum/153-which-joysticks-work-with-the-c64-mini-my-list.txt

Supported Joysticks (Firmware > 1.0.6.):

- 8Bitdo SFC30 GamePad; Zero GamePad
- Afterglow Wired Controller for Xbox One
- DragonRise Inc. Generic USB Joystick
- EA Sports PS3 Controller
- GameCube {HuiJia USB box};{WiseGroup USB box}
- GameStop Gamepad
- Generic X-Box pad
- Goodbetterbest Ltd USB Controller
- Gravis GamePad Pro USB
- GreenAsia Inc. USB Joystick
- HitBox (PS3/PC) Analog Mode

- HJC Game GAMEPAD

- HORI CO. LTD. FIGHTING STICK 3; REAL ARCADE Pro.V3

- Hori Pad EX Turbo 2

- iBuffalo USB 2-axis 8-button Gamepad

- InterAct GoPad I-73000 (Fighting Game Layout)

- JC-U3613M - DirectInput Mode

- Jess Technology USB Game Controller

- Logic3 Controller

- Logitech Cordless RumblePad 2

- Logitech F310 Gamepad (DInput); (XInput); F510 Gamepad (XInput); F710 Gamepad (DInput); (XInput)

- Logitech Dual Action; RumblePad 2 USB; WingMan Cordless RumblePad

- Mad Catz C.T.R.L.R; Fightpad SFxT; Wired Xbox 360 Controller; Xbox 360 Controller

- Microntek USB Joystick; Xbox Gamepad (userspace driver)

- Microsoft X-Box 360 pad; One pad; One pad v2; Pad (Japan); Pad v2 (US); X360 Controller; Wireless Controller

- Moga Pro

- NEXT Classic USB Game Controller

- Nintendo Wii U Pro Controller; Wiimote

- OUYA Game Controller

- PC Game Controller

- PS3 Controller & (Bluetooth)

- Razer Onza Classic Edition; Tournament

- Retro Games LTD THEC64 Joystick; The64 Joystick Prototype

- Retrolink Classic Controller; Saturn Classic Controller

- RetroUSB.com RetroPad; Super RetroPort

- Rock Candy Gamepad for PS3; Wired Controller for Xbox One

- Saitek Cyborg V.1 Game Pad; P2900 Wireless Pad; P880; PLC Saitek P3200 Rumble Pad

- Sony DualShock 4; DualShock 4 BT; DualShock 4 V2; DualShock 4 V2 BT; DualShock 4 Wireless Adaptor

- Sony PS2 pad with SmartJoy adapter

- Speedlink TORID Wireless Gamepad

- Speedlink XEOX Pro Analog Gamepad pad

- Super Joy Box 5 Pro

- Thrustmaster 2 in 1 DT; Dual Analog 4; Dual Trigger 3-in-1; Firestorm Dual Power; Run N Drive Wireless (PS3)

- Tomee SNES USB Controller

- Toodles 2008 Chimp PC/PS3

- Twin USB PS2 Adapter

- USB Gamepad; GamepadChris

- Valve Streaming Gamepad

- VR-BOX

5.2.2 4-player mode

See also: 10 Games & downloads, 5.4 USB hub, 10.6 4-joystick games

Question: Is 4 player gaming possible?

Retro Games: The current firmware does not allow it but we are hoping to add this in future firmware updates.

Nevertheless and for future purposes I added some useful information and links for this feature under chapter 10.6 4-joystick games

5.2.3 Arduino joystick (or adaptor)

I will quickly show how to create an Arduino based C64 joystick for the Mini. I will assume you already know a bit about Arduino and require little to no help when attaching the joystick to your Arduino board.

I can't remember which joystick library I used, but there seems to be a handful of them and it looks like they all work exactly the same way.

For this particular joystick, I will be using the auto fire switch to toggle between normal and 'extra button' mode. In normal mode, The joystick will work as you'd expect. With Up, Down, Left, Right, Fire1 and Fire2 representing those functions. In 'extra button' mode, Fire1 = button 3, Fire2 = button 4, Up = button 5, Down = button 6, Left = button 7 and Right = button 8. This allows us to use the full functionality of the Mini without needing the original joystick.

Here is the code: http://thec64community.online/thread/102/arduino-joystick-adaptor

I used pins 6,2,3,7,8,9,10 for my joystick, you can use whatever you want. I only used those pins because my Arduino was damaged and some pins don't work.

For this to work, you need an Arduino with one of the Atmega32U2 or Atmega32U4. I used an Arduino Leonardo clone called pro micro. Once you have the joystick wired up and the sketch uploaded, you can test it in windows if you like, just to make sure.

For the finishing touch, you need to add the joystick layout to the Mini. The file you need to edit is - \usr\share\the64\ui\data\gamecontrollerdb.txt. Simply add the following line to the end of the file.

```
03000000041230000368000000101010000,Arduino LLC
Arduino Leonardo,a:b4,b:b5,x:b3,y:b2,back:b6,
start:b7,lefttrigger:b0,righttrigger:b1,leftx
:a0,lefty:a1,platform:Linux,
```

I currently don't know how to add this directly on the Mini, I'm using the USB boot method at the moment.

So that's it, you can use your old C64 joystick on the Mini without losing functionality.

```
#include <joystick.h>
// Use whichever pins you like, I used these
because some of the other pins were damaged.
// I will be using the auto fire switch on my
zipstick to emulate the last 6 buttons on the
joystick.
// up, down, left, right, fire1, fire2, auto
switch
char myPin[]={6, 2, 3, 7, 8, 9, 10};
// Set up the Arduino as an 8-button gamepad.
Joystick_ Joystick(JOYSTICK_DEFAULT_REPORT_
ID,JOYSTICK_TYPE_GAMEPAD,
8, 0, // Button Count, Hat Switch Count
true, true, false, // X and Y, but no Z Axis
false, false, false, // No Rx, Ry, or Rz
false, false, // No rudder or throttle
false, false, false); // No accelerator,
brake, or steering
//------------------------[ Button handling,
very accurate ]------------------------
#define HELD 0
#define NEW 1
#define RELEASE 2
byte CompletePad, ExPad, TempPad, myPad;
bool _A[3], _B[3], _C[3], _Up[3], _Down[3],
_Left[3], _Right[3];
void UPDATEPAD(int pad, int var) {
_C[pad] = (var >> 1)&1;
_B[pad] = (var >> 2)&1;
_A[pad] = (var >> 3)&1;
_Down[pad] = (var >> 4)&1;
_Left[pad] = (var >> 5)&1;
_Right[pad] = (var >> 6)&1;
_Up[pad] = (var >> 7)&1;
}
byte updateButtons(byte var){
var = 0;
if (!digitalRead(myPin[6])) var |= (1<<1);
```

```
if (!digitalRead(myPin[5])) var |= (1<<2);
if (!digitalRead(myPin[4])) var |= (1<<3); //
P1_9 = A
if (!digitalRead(myPin[1])) var |= (1<<4);
if (!digitalRead(myPin[2])) var |= (1<<5);
if (!digitalRead(myPin[3])) var |= (1<<6);
if (!digitalRead(myPin[0])) var |= (1<<7);
return var;
}
void UpdatePad(int joy_code){
ExPad = CompletePad;
CompletePad = joy_code;
UPDATEPAD(HELD, CompletePad); // held
UPDATEPAD(RELEASE, (ExPad & (~CompletePad)));
// released
UPDATEPAD(NEW, (CompletePad & (~ExPad))); //
newpress
}
//-----------------------------------------
-------------------------------------------
void setup() {
// Initialize Button Pins
Serial.begin(9600);
for (int index = 0; index < sizeof(myPin);
index++)
{
pinMode(myPin[index], INPUT_PULLUP);
}
// Initialize Joystick Library
Joystick.begin();
Joystick.setXAxisRange(-1, 1);
Joystick.setYAxisRange(-1, 1);
}
void loop() {
// update buttons
myPad = updateButtons(myPad);
UpdatePad(myPad);
```

```
if(_C[HELD]){ // if 'autofire' then use
fire1,2,up,down,left,right as extra buttons!
if(_A[HELD]){
Joystick.setButton(2, 1);
}else{
Joystick.setButton(2, 0);
}
if(_B[HELD]){
Joystick.setButton(3, 1);
}else{
Joystick.setButton(3, 0);
}
if(_Up[HELD]){
Joystick.setButton(4, 1);
}else{
Joystick.setButton(4, 0);
}
if(_Down[HELD]){
Joystick.setButton(5, 1);
}else{
Joystick.setButton(5, 0);
}
if(_Left[HELD]){
Joystick.setButton(6, 1);
}else{
Joystick.setButton(6, 0);
}
if(_Right[HELD]){
Joystick.setButton(7, 1);
}else{
Joystick.setButton(7, 0);
}
}else{ // if not autofire, then use the joy-
stick as normal
if(_Up[HELD]){
Joystick.setYAxis(-1);
}else if(_Down[HELD]){
Joystick.setYAxis(1);
```

```
}else{
Joystick.setYAxis(0);
}
if(_Left[HELD]){
Joystick.setXAxis(-1);
}else if(_Right[HELD]){
Joystick.setXAxis(1);
}else{
Joystick.setXAxis(0);
}
if(_A[HELD]){
Joystick.setButton(0, 1);
}else{
Joystick.setButton(0, 0);
}
if(_B[HELD]){
Joystick.setButton(1, 1);
}else{
Joystick.setButton(1, 0);
}
}
}
```

5.2.4 Arduino joystick USB

There is nothing better than real hardware.

With this board and software, you can connect your old C64 joystick to your computer USB port in about 5 minutes and play your favourite games like in the 80s.

Once everything is hooked map the joystick buttons as follows: UP (w), DOWN (s), LEFT (a), RIGHT (d) and BUTTON (q) and you'll be good to go.

The Arduino board will act as a keyboard and each joystick movement triggers a keystroke.

Follow this link to read more! https://create.arduino.cc/projecthub/fpfaffendorf/commodore-64-joystick-usb-adapter-c64joy-fc2389?ref=tag&ref_id=joystick&offset=11

5.3 Keyboard

See also: 3.9 64 Doctor

TIP: For using a keyboard, two joysticks and an USB-stick, use a keyboard with at least two building USB-ports.

Virtual keyboard using tip:

You can easily swap from the letter section to the number section and then to the special sign section by pressing the left triangle button. The cursor then always jumps to the first sign in the left corner of each section.

The keyboard mapping (by Retro Games):

Ensure you have selected the layout on the Mini relevant for your USB keyboard. Also, choose the corresponding option below before reading the remainder of these instructions, as each keyboard layout is different from the next. For example, if your keyboard is US, then choose the US option on the USB keyboard screen on the Mini and the US option below.

Introduction

Generally, the letter and number keys on an USB keyboard do what you expect them to when connected to the Mini. However, the original computer has other keys that you won't find on a modern USB keyboard; RUN STOP and RESTORE being two examples.

Function keys

Firstly, look at the function keys section below. Note that the 'change color' options are only relevant when you are in C64 BASIC and that you have to press both keys shown against the function. Other keys include some of those exclusive C64 keys mentioned in the introduction. So, when a game says to press RESTORE you will know which key to press on your USB keyboard by referring to this list.

HOME/CLEAR	Home
DELETE	⌫
INSERT	Insert
RESTORE	Tab ⇆
RUN/STOP	Esc
RETURN	↵
CURSOR UP	↑
CURSOR DOWN	↓
CURSOR LEFT	←
CURSOR RIGHT	→
SPACE	Space
F1	F1
F2	F2

F3	F3
F4	F4
F5	F5
F6	F6
F7	F7
F8	F8
Change color to BLACK	Ctrl ! 1
Change color to WHITE	Ctrl @ 2
Change color to RED	Ctrl # 3
Change color to CYAN	Ctrl $ 4
Change color to PURPLE	Ctrl % 5
Change color to GREEN	Ctrl ^ 6
Change color to BLUE	Ctrl & 7

Change color to YELLOW	Ctrl * 8
Change color to ORANGE	⊞ ! 1
Change color to BROWN	⊞ @ 2
Change color to LIGHT RED	⊞ # 3
Change color to DARK GRAY	⊞ $ 4
Change color to MEDIUM GRAY	⊞ % 5
Change color to LIGHT GREEN	⊞ ^ 6
Change color to LIGHT BLUE	⊞ & 7
Change color to LIGHT GRAY	⊞ * 8
REVERSE ON	Ctrl (9
REVERSE OFF	Ctrl) 0

Modifier keys

Next are the Modifier keys. If a game's instructions tell you to press the CTRL (or Control) key, then you will know what to do by referring to the information here.

Letters/numbers

Letters/numbers are usually nice and simple. However, things are a little more complex if you are using certain programs or are in C64 BASIC, where they recognize the difference between an upper case and a lower-case character. By default, C64 BASIC begins in 'uppercase/graphic mode', in which the character on the left is shown. The other mode is 'upper- and lower-case mode', which shows the character displayed on the right. When playing a game, you won't have to switch modes so you don't need to worry about this.

To switch between these two modes, press ⊞ and `Shift` together.

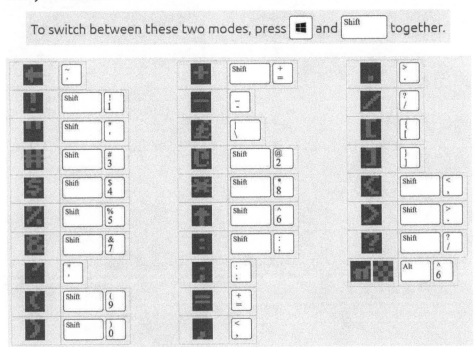

Typographical symbols

Next we have typographical symbols including all the commas, brackets and punctuation characters. For most of these, you press the keys you would normally expect.

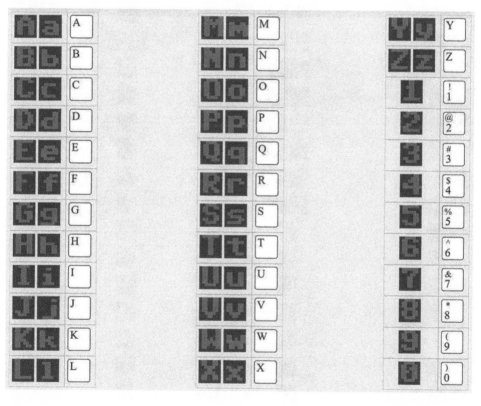

Graphical Symbols

Lastly, we have the graphics symbols, which are of most interest to programmers. If you are only going to play games or run programs written by others, you are unlikely to need to know these key presses. You need to be in C64 BASIC to see these symbols appear.

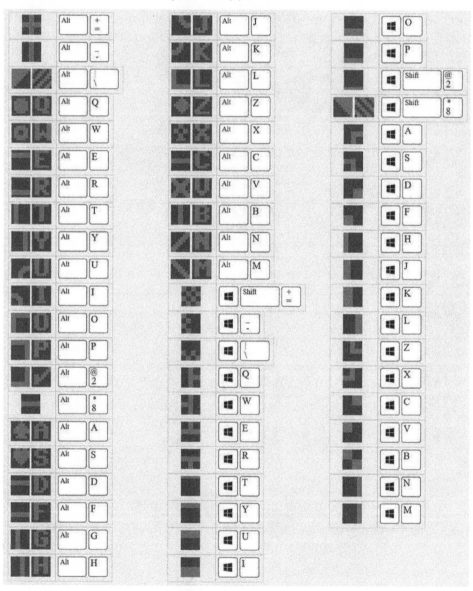

5.3.1 USB keyboards

In principle, almost any USB keyboard can be used. The keys can be mapped, i.e. assigned differently, in order to come close to the original C64 keyboard or to offer its functions.

ATTENTION & TIP: A keyboard with a built-in USB hub offers the nice possibility to connect more than two devices to the Mini. Yet, it also has the disadvantage that most of these keyboards do not have, an external power supply. Therefore, the other USB ports may not provide enough power to support e.g. additional USB sticks. joysticks that potentially require little or no power are no problem.

Problems may also occur if an illuminated keyboard is used. In this case, a power supply that is too small can supply too little power to the Mini and results in it switching off.

5.3.2 Using the original keyboard!

In this section, I present two possibilities to use an original C64 keyboard with the Mini.

5.3.2.1 Keyrah

With Keyrah, you can connect keyboards of classic computers to modern computers via USB. Two joystick ports are also available and the movements are converted to keystrokes. The following operating systems are supported: Linux, Windows or Mac PC, Raspberry Pi.

With Keyrah, V2 you can use the keyboards of all other C64 versions / the VC20 / C16 / C116 / C128 & (D) as well as Amiga 600 and 1200!

Simply plug it in via USB and you're done.

Keyrah with keyboard:

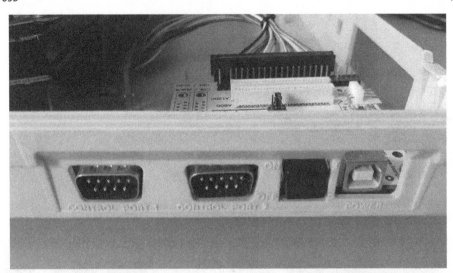

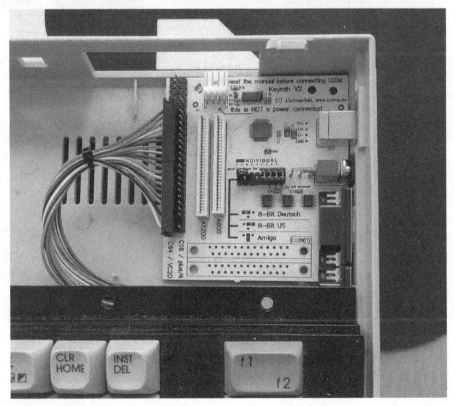

The YouTube link shows how to use the Keyrah. https://www.youtube.com/watch?v=7AvdcD3V0Sg

5.3.2.2 C64KEYS2USB

The USB adapter was conceived and implemented by Thorsten Kattanek.

However, it is currently not available as a finished version that you can buy. You'll have to do it yourself and solder it together.

Over this link http://www.emu64-projekt.de/forum/index.php?page=Att achment&attachmentID=992 you will find the file in which all necessary information is available to get started (to download the file, you have to register at http://www.emu64-projekt.de (Free).

Here is a YouTube video where you can see how it works. https://youtu.be/ Al8iKusKVjw

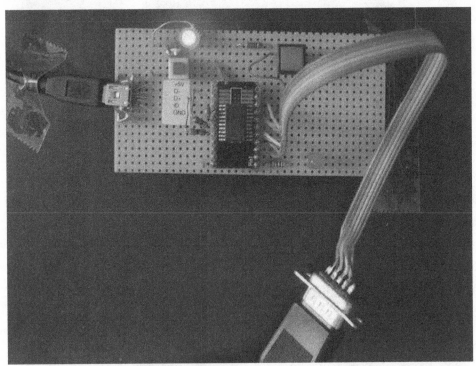

5.3.3 Connecting the SX64 keyboard

Commodore's SX-64 was a portable color computer based on the tech-nology of the legendary C64. In addition, it has a wonderfully designed external keyboard. Fortunately, there is a solution to use it with the Mini.

This was provided by Jim Brain at Retro Innovations. http://store.go4retro.com/c-key-keyboard-adapter/

All you need is this wonderful adapter and after you can use the keyboard for your PC as well!

More to read is via this link: http://armchairarcade.com/perspectives/2016/05/15/review-commodore-sx-64-keyboard-replacement-solution-plus-64jpx-red/

5.4 USB hub

See also: 5.2.2 4-player mode, 4.4 Power supply

A USB keyboard, joystick and USB stick need together about 0.150 Ampere.

The Mini needs about 1 Ampere. Hence, for this configuration there is no need for an active powered USB hub.

Thus, a HUB with e.g. 4 ports without an extra power supply is completely sufficient.

5.5 DB9/Sub-D/D-Sub USB joystick adapter

There are many different adapter solutions to connect old joysticks with DB9 or SUB D connectors which you can use to play. There is a chance that not all of them will work. Search THEC64 Mini communities for tips.

Here is a Google search to find them "joystick+adapter+DB9+or+SUBD"

5.5.1 *TOM* USB Mouse-Joystick Adapter

Mouse / Joystick / Gamepad / Keyboard (as Mouse/Gamepad Emulator) for Retro Computers!

Adapter Features

Connect most mouse / gamepads / joysticks or keyboards to your retro computer via USB Socket - wired or with wireless receiver.

Support for most Amiga, Atari ST / Falcon / TT and C=64 / C=128. Easily re-configurable (no need to open case just use your mouse - setting stored).

No need to install any drivers or programs on above OS.

Works perfectly with most mouse's including wireless, tested on: Workbench, TOS and GEOS.

Hot plug - just plug or swap your favourite device any time.

Use both connected mouse and keyboard on one dongle - mouse to move cursor on your OS and keyboard to play your favourite games.

Configure your favourite buttons for gamepad / joystick - up to 10 reconfigurable buttons - including auto-fire for button 1 and 2.

Amiga CD32 games supported - play games with up to 7 buttons.

Emulating mouse on gamepad / joystick.

Connect most known PSX gamepad to our adapter.

More to read is on eBay! Search for: https://www.ebay.co.uk/itm/TOM-USB-Mouse-Joystick-Adapter-for-Commodore-C-64-C-128-AMIGA-ATARI-ST-TT-/172007029169?hash=item280c6af9b1:g:2YEAAOSwcBhWUcBE

or search for "TOM-USB-Mouse-Joystick-Adapter-for-Commodore-C-64-C-128-AMIGA-ATARI-ST-TT"

5.5.2 C64 USB joystick adapter

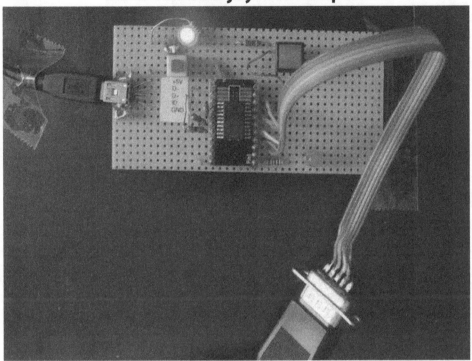

There are some nice emulators for vintage video games and computers out there. For example, the WinVICE for Commodore Hardware like the C64. But how do you connect old joysticks to your PC, like the Competition Pro (the original one, with 9-pin D-sub for an original C64, not the USB version)? Most emulators provide joystick emulation with the cursor keys or other configurable keys. Thus, this project is one solution for this problem which is a Freescale Microcontroller that implements an USB keyboard and translates the up/down ect. buttons to keyboard events, as if you have pressed the cursor keys.

More to read is on the webpage! http://www.instructables.com/id/C64-USB-Joystick-Adapter/

5.5.2.1 eMail Author Frank Buss

mailto:fb@frank-buss.de

5.5.3 aJoy USB adapter

The aJoy nano joystick USB adapter allows the easy connection of digital retro joysticks and joypads through the USB Interface of modern PCs.

Relive the play experience with an original joystick or gamepad!

Nearly every joystick from the 80s can be used with this adapter furthermore.

For the Mini as well as many others are compatible with the following operating systems:

Windows 98 / XP / Vista / 7/8, Mac OSX, Linux, RetroPie (Raspberry Pi) and more.

More to read is on the webpage! http://16xeight.de/index.php/shop/product/view/1/8

5.5.3.1 eMail Author Daniel Müller

mailto:info@dcm-pc.de

5.5.4 Competition Pro retro joystick USB adapter

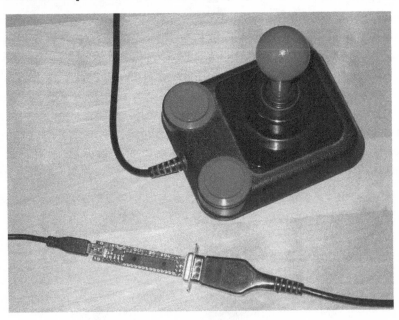

This small adapter allows you to connect a vintage joystick via USB.

The schematic is very simple:

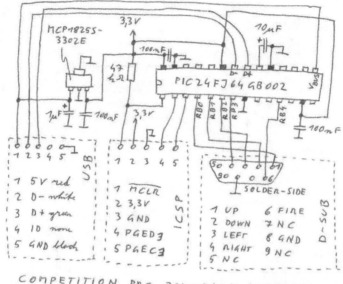

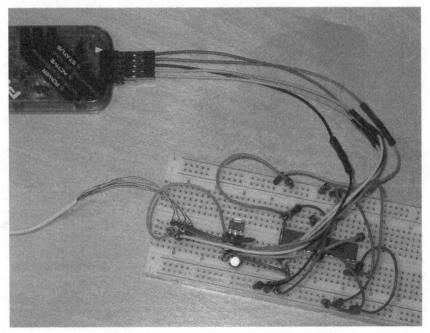

After prototyping the circuit on a breadboard

the parts onto a perfboard

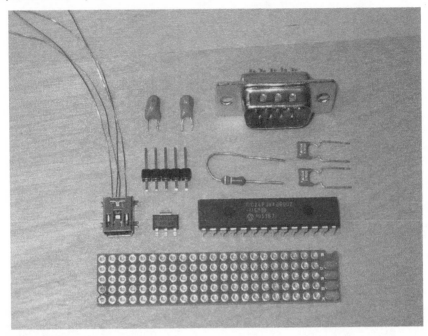

and the interconnections were made by using some isolated relay wire.

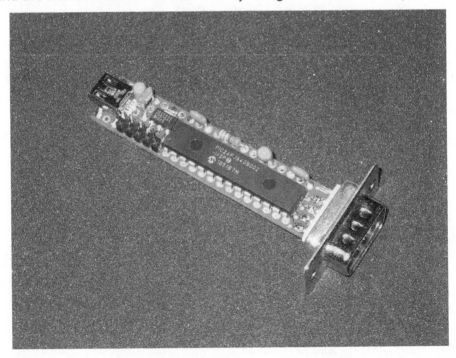

Please find the firmware attached.

Have fun, Markus

P.S.: Helpful resources about USB HID are here:

http://de.wikipedia.org/wiki/Competition_Pro

http://vice-emu.sourceforge.net/

http://www.engscope.com/pic24-tutorial/14-4-usb-hid-joystick/

http://frank.circleofcurrent.com/cache/hid_tutorial_1.htm

More to read is on the webpage! http://dangerousprototypes.com/forum/viewtopic.php?f=56&t=2971

5.5.5 JoyDivision joystick adapter

This adapter was created because I missed being able to control my old games in emulators with a real controller (Joysticks), just as they were intended to be played =)

This adapter is created as a HID that doesn't require any specific drivers (thanks to V-USB which is used). That means that you just need to plug it in, configure your Emulator to use the HID-Device and start playing!

One other nifty thing we added to it (also from V-USB package) is that this unit contains a special Bootloader which enables the User to update/replace the firmware without having a special programmer and only an USB-port and use a software called HIDBootFlash (read more about this procedure below). Having this Bootloader enabled means that one can change the firmware to its own needs.

We plan to add firmware for other input devices (like Amiga and Atari mice's ect.). The archive contains source code (firmware and Bootloader), Schematics, BOM and EAGLE-files.

We also shared the PCB-layout (if someone wants to build it themselves) at https://oshpark.com/shared_projects/eoh7Ay5p.

There's more to read on the webpage! http://www.onyxsoft.se/joydivision.html

5.5.6 USB 2 D-Sub adapter rys_mkii

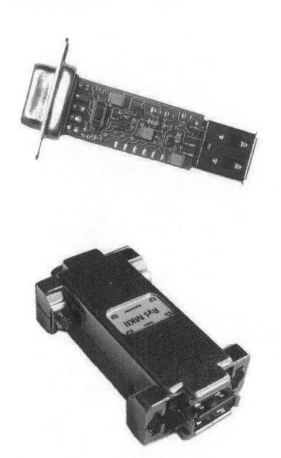

List of projects / Ryś MKII Adapter

Ryś MK II Adapter comes as a successor to Ryś USB. Similar to its predecessor, it is based on a 16-bit Microchip Microcontroller and it can be used together with USB HID devices like mouses, joysticks, pads.

Our product provides built-in USB stack which enables USB HID devices (like a mouse, a joystick or a pad) support without the need for installing additional software drivers. Ryś's installation procedure consists of simply plugging it into the correct port (i.e. mouse- or joystick-port) into one's computer.

Ryś MK II has been equipped with 3 modes of emulation: one for a mouse, another for a joystick and the last one for a pad. Mouse emulation comes with 3 user-definable tracking speed options. This feature allows you to match just the right speed for the particular device being connected. All these preferences are saved to the built-in EEPROM Memory. Thanks to this, when you reconnect the device it is now already configured! Ryś also comes with "Bootloader" function that facilitates future firmware upgrades.

Features of Ryś

- support for mouses using both USB HID and USB-PS/2

- support for USB HID joysticks

- support for USB HID pads

- support for both USB HID and USB-PS/2 keyboards

- ready to use with every Amiga (although some models may require additional adapters)

- ready to use with Commodore 64 (without support for mouse)

- ready for use with Atari ST (require additional adapters)

- built-in USB stack

- "Bootloader" function facilitating future firmware upgrades

- LED "Status" indicator providing information about device's state

- built-in EEPROM Memory enabling storage of user preferences

- built around 16-bit Microchip Microcontroller utilizing nanoWatt technology

- 3 mouse emulation modes,

- Joystick mode (emulating original joystick behavior)

- pad mode (emulating original pad behavior)

- CD32 pad mode (original CD32 pad emulation mode)

Ryś automatically detects the type of connected Device and starts emulation of its original Amiga counterpart.

When our Device finds a joystick or a pad, it automatically switches into a pad mode. When one connects a joystick, he or she should change Ryś's operating mode for joystick mode by simultaneously pressing joystick's keys 9 and 10. If the command succeeds it will be confirmed by the blinking of the LED 'Status' indicator. Similar operation should be performed when a pad is connected. After, one should simultaneously press "SELECT" and "START" buttons (sometimes referred to as "9" and "10").

Functions of Ryś

Mouse

- "Bootloader" + wheel button – emulation mode selection

Joystick

- 9 + 10 - choosing operation mode
- "Bootloader" + 4 - choosing operation mode
- 1 - fire1
- 2 - fire2
- 3 - fire3
- 6 - autofire1
- 5 - autofire2

Pad

- SELECT + START - choosing operation mode
- X - fire1
- O - fire2
- [] - UP
- R2 - autofire1
- L2 - autofire2

Keyboard

- F1-F2 - choosing operation mode

Change of adapter's operating mode is being signaled by the blinking of the LED "Status" indicator.

When a joystick or a pad is connected:

- 1 blink – "Joystick" mode
- 2 blinks – "Pad" mode
- 3 blinks – "Pad - mouse emulation" mode
- 4 blinks – CD32 pad mode

When a mouse is connected:

- 4 blinks – tracking speed change
- "Bootloader" button + left/right mouse button – mouse speed adjustment

When a keyboard is connected:

- F1 function key - (A-left, W-up, S-down, D-right, O-fire1, P-fire2)
- F2 function key - (left arrow key, right arrow key, down arrow key, up arrow key, W-fire1, Q-fire2)

More to read is on the webpage! http://retro.7-bit.pl/?lang=en&go=projekty&name=rys_mkii

5.6 Mouse

See also: 3.7 Operating systems

Using a mouse is currently not supported.

It may be possible for future firmware but it's not a definite yes.

5.7 Lightpen

For the C64 and others of its kind, there was the Lightpen, which is nothing more than a photodiode that is held in front of the screen and moved. The lightpen's electronics then convert the incoming beams from the screen into signals for the joystick-port. With the use of a software a cross will then be displayed on the screen. A small button on the pen allows a click to be triggered and functions could be controlled. Modern screens no longer work with cathode ray technology. Moreover, they do not build up an image with an energy beam that allows control of the pen. Therefore, a Lightpen cannot be used on the Mini.

You can find more information if you follow this link: https://www.c64-wiki.com/wiki/Light_pen

6 Modding

Modding or Modden, is among other things the opening and rebuilding of a computer with simple changes like a reset button or CPU brake, or could go as far wherein the actual computer is no longer recognizable. The loss of warranty had to be accepted.

With this google search you can find some examples worth seeing! "C64+modding"

6.1 Raspberry Pi

VMAX Dirk did a small modification and installed a Raspberry Pi in the Mini: https://www.facebook.com/groups/209280506324242/permalink/216918578893768/

Hence, the bridge is built to get the best of both worlds. On one hand, you have the unlimited storage space and the option to have all games at once in presented one list and on one medium. While on the other hand you have the case of the Mini as well as its functionalities.

At any rate it is a good approach to experiment with the conversion of a Mini.

6.2 Adding a MicroSD port

Gurce has started to connect a MicroSD port to the Mini.

At https://twitter.com/Gurcelsikyildiz you can follow him up on this project.

By now it's only an idea and not working.

Here are some insights on his findings:

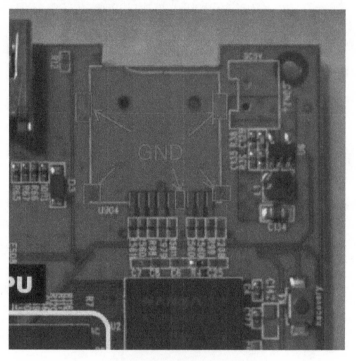

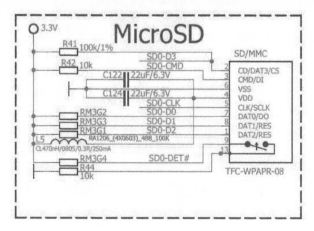

6.3 PAL <> NTSC

There is no way to change the PAL Version to NTSC or make it appear as one. The board must be replaced for this to happen.

The only other alternative so far is a HDMI PAL to NTSC Converter which you can get for a small cost on Amazon or eBay.

But the best solution is to buy the NTSC or PAL Mini Version.

Here is the corresponding Google search entry: "HDMI+PAL+to+NTSC+Converter"

6.4 TV out

If you want to connect the Mini to an old TV with SCART connector, then there are ready-made converters that are suitable for this.

Unfortunately, I didn't find one that converts HDMI to the good old FBAS TV-analog signal.

Here is the corresponding Google search entry: "HDMI+TV+scart+converter"

6.5 Audio out

If you like to connect your Mini to your home sound equipment, the easiest way is a HDMI audio converter. It splits the audio signal out of the HDMI-Stream and you get the sound on jack plugs.

Here is a Google search of it: "hdmi+audio+extractor"

6.6 THEC64 Mini Portable

There is a very neat little project to transform the Mini into some sort of Laptop to make it portable and independent from a mounted power source.

Click this Link to watch the video on YouTube. https://www.youtube.com/watch?v=HP0JAJZKlpQ

6.7 THEC64 Mini inside a real C64

Perifractic from Retro Recipes has built a C64 with a THEC64 Mini inside.

All he needed was a soldering iron, a Keyrah and a spare original C64 Case.

Here's how he did it: https://youtu.be/4f3pzuZA2As

7 Hacks

Hint! Changes to the hardware, as well as the software (apart from e.g. the installation of a new firmware), you do at your own risk with the possibility of legal consequences.

7.1 The operating system

The Mini is running with a Linux based operating system.

This chapter will show you how to use some nifty tools to get deep into the Mini.

7.1.1 C64Mini FEL-mode hack - no UART needed.

This text in its original form, was created by jj0 Jeroen, who gave me permission for use in this book.

From (mostly) the source released by Retro LTD, I've created a kernel+ramdisk that you can use to boot the C64Mini from via FEL mode. I've included:

- An on-screen command shell that allows you to do all the command-line stuff from an USB keyboard. So, opening up the Mini should not be necessary anymore.
- Support for a number of USB2Serial converters (CP210x, FTDI, Prolific 2302). You can insert an USB2Serial converter in one of the Mini's USB ports and connect the RX/TX/GND to either a second USB2Serial converter on a PC, or directly to TTL-level serial port on e.g. a Raspberry PI, Cubieboard, etc.
- Support for a number of USB2Ethernet devices (ASIX AS88xxx, QF9700, SMSC LAN75XX and LAN95XX). If you insert one of these in the Mini's USB port and connect it with your router (using an Ethernet cable) it will get an IP address. Supported services are SSH, SCP and/or ftp.
- The UART is also still supported.
- Running scripts from an inserted USB drive. If the USB drive has a directory 'scripts', each file in this directory will be run as if it were a Linux shell script. So, you can do unattended copies etc. I've included two example scripts. One that backs up the nand firmware and one that copies games from a 'copygames' folder to the Mini.

- root password is 'manicminerrules!'

The required files can be found in https://github.com/jj-0/C64Mini-FEL-boot/blob/master/C64Mini-FEL-boot-v1.zip. If you unzip the file, you will have the following folders:

- boot: This contains the required kernel, script.bin etc. files.
- USB: Example 'scripts' and 'copygames' to put on an USB-Stick.
- linux: sunxi-fel tool for linux (x86_64) and boot.sh to upload the kernel etc. to the Mini. If the tools don't work you might need to install them yourself (apt-get sunxi-tools) or compile them from source http://linux-sunxi.org/Sunxi-tools.
- windows: sunxi-fel tool and dll's for Windows (64-bit) and boot.sh to upload the kernel etc. to the Mini. If the tools don't work, then googling is your best friend. I don't know too much about compiling this on Windows.

To use this:
Examine the USB directory and put the content in the root of an USB drive, if you want to use scripts. Look at the scripts in the 'scripts-examples' directory and if you want to use them, put them in the scripts folder of the USB drive. You can also leave this out, or do it later, or write your own scripts.

Then you have to start your C64 Mini in FEL mode http://linux-sunxi.org/FEL. Insert a (fully-functioning data-cable, so not just for power) USB cable in the Mini's micro-USB port. Before inserting the other side into your PC (or for ease of use, use an USB hub that lets you switch ports on and off):

- If you have an UART connected keep '2' pressed and insert the USB cable into your PC/switch the USB port on. But that kind of defeats the purpose, though it's still kind of useful.
- There's a button 'hidden' underneath the silver sticker on the underside of the Mini. Keep this pressed and then insert the USB cable into your PC and switch the USB port on.

!Attention! This however, will only work if you have a Mini with silver-label at the bottom. If you have the newer version, without the silver-label, you will need to either attach a button to the appropriate port on the board or solder one in yourself. This requires opening up the case and your warranty is gone. But because you need the switch it's needed to be done to use this trick.

Once you've done either of these, your PC should have a new USB device (1f3a:efe8, on my Ubuntu PC it's called an 'Onda (unverified) V972 tablet in flashing mode').

Next

- If you're using Linux, cd to the linux folder and run ./boot.sh
- If you're using Windows 7 or 10 (64 bit) cd to the windows folder and run boot.cmd. You might need to install an USB driver (http://linux-sunxi.org/FEL/USBBoot#Mandatory_USB_driver). But if you have hackchi2 installed the driver might already be installed.

If all works well you will see that the kernel etc. files are being uploaded:

```
USB device 001:040 Allwinner A20 xxxxxxxx:xxx
xxxxx:xxxxxxx:xxxxxxxx
Stack pointers: sp_irq=0x00002000,
sp=0x00005E08
Reading the MMU translation table from
0x00020000
Disabling I-cache, MMU and branch predic-
tion... done.
=> Executing the SPL... done.
Setting write-combine mapping for DRAM.
```

```
Setting cached mapping for BROM.
Writing back the MMU translation table.
Enabling I-cache, MMU and branch predic-
tion... done.
Writing image "U-Boot 2018.05-jj_0+ for sunxi
b", 372007 bytes @ 0x4A000000.
Passing boot info via sunxi SPL: script ad-
dress = 0x43100000, uEnv length = 260
Starting U-Boot (0x4A000000).
```

Then you will see activity on screen (a.o. u-boot starting and booting the kernel) and after ~35 seconds you should end up with an on-screen command-line shell, where you can type away at your leisure with an attached USB keyboard. If you have a supported USB2Serial device attached there, will also be a command-line shell on that and also on the UART. If you have a supported USB2Ethernet device attached, you should see a 'c64mini' in your router's list of devices as well. The on-screen shell prompt should also show the IP address between brackets:

```
root@c64mini(10.0.0.125):/#
```

At this point (unless you've run some of the scripts), your Mini is just another small-board computer and nothing has touched the actual 'C64Mini' contents. However, after you load the nand driver (included from the C64Mini firmware version 1.2.0) you have access to the Mini's root filesystem and can modify it at will:

```
root@c64mini (10.0.0.125):/#insmod -f /opt/
nand.ko
root@c64mini (10.0.0.125):/#mount /dev/nandb
/mnt
```

That's it. Have fun!

Please note that I'm not responsible for ANYTHING you do with your C64Mini, everything you do is at your own risk. I recommend that you, first of all, make a backup of the nand before doing anything else.

7.1.2 UART Interface Root access

See also: 4.3 Pin assignment & buttons

For inserting games directly into the Mini without using an USB-stick, you need to do is this hardware/software hack.

If you want to do any major customization to the Mini, one of the first things you will need to do is add the UART connector so you can gain access to the internal software. You'll need basic soldering skills and a simple soldering iron that you can get from almost any electronics store. I wouldn't recommend anything more than a 30w iron otherwise you might damage the delicate copper tracks. Soldering takes a bit to perfect. All I can say is: always dab a little solder on the tip first, then make sure the tip sits on both the pin you are soldering and the pad you want the solder to flow on. Then feed the solder on steady and with only just enough to make the bond. I always try to make sure this action is done in no more than 5 seconds or you may damage the delicate copper tracks.

What you'll need:

USB to 3.3v TTL RS232 adaptor. It MUST use 3.3v for the Tx line. Be careful as some are 5v and may damage your Mini! Use a multimeter to confirm. I bought this from eBay "PL2303HX-USB-To-TTL-RS232-UART-Auto-Converter-To-COM-Cable-Adapter-Module-AU"

Soldering iron with fine pointed tip (fine chisel will also do)

Multimeter (Optional but recommended to test the Tx line of your adaptor)

Solder (60/40 and thin diameter, maybe .7 or so)

Header pins that you can snap off. This is what I bought and snapped off a row of four.

Start:

Open up the 64 Mini by turning it over and peeling off the four rubber feet. After, remove the exposed screws.

Gently pull the two connectors off the PCB that go to the power led and the switch on the bottom of the case.

Undo the screws that hold the PCB to the bottom section of the case.

Locate the four through holes on the PCB, just near the A20 chip, these connections are for the serial UART. Here is where you will solder on to the short ends of your PCB connector that will be sticking through.

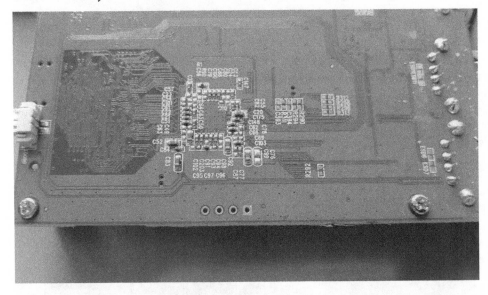

Place the longer section of the four PCB pins on the side that has no chips on it and solder in place. Once finished, put the PCB back in place and put the screws back in.

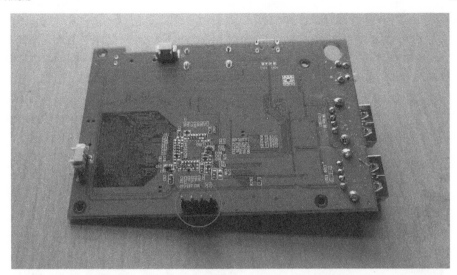

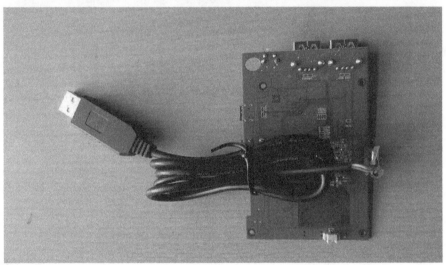

Following the instructions that came with your USB to TTL converter, install drivers (if required) and connect to a free USB port and the serial connections to the UART pins you just installed. You will need to make the connections like this:

64Mini UART / USB TTL Adapter:
GND / GND
Tx / Rx
Rx / Tx
3.3v / None

Download PuTTY https://www.chiark.greenend.org.uk/~sgtatham/putty/ latest.html or some other serial terminal program and set the baud rate to 115200 and data format 8,n,1. Com port will be dependent on your particular setup. Mine was Com3 according to device manager.

Make sure you select 'Serial' so you can enter these values in.

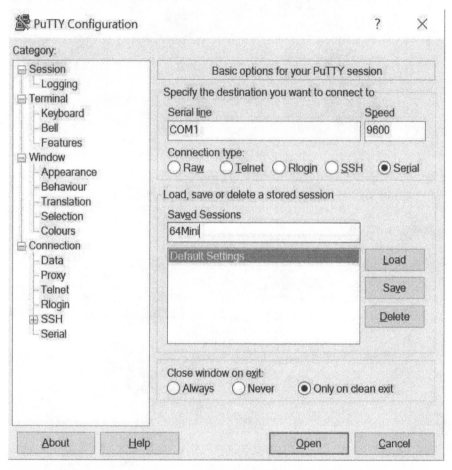

Connect your Mini to HDMI and power. If you have done everything correctly, you should be seeing the console output in the terminal program window!

Getting into the U-boot prompt

The Mini does not need to be connected to a TV or monitor, you only need Putty to connect to it and UART of course... :)

The next step is a bit complex because you have to do 2 things at the same time. The easiest way is to ask a friend or someone in your household shortly for help (to press a key on the keyboard "s"). Or find some way to do it yourself…

You must now select your terminal window and hold down the "s" key on your PC keyboard. Then, supply the Mini using the micro USB plug with power. This stops the boot process of the Mini. Remember, as soon as the UART adapter is connected to the Mini you can no longer use the power button to turn it off / on. If it did not work the first time, you just have to unplug the power, plug it in again. Repeat if necessary.

If not, check that the connections are correct (i.e. that you haven't connected Tx to Tx and Rx to Rx) and check that your terminal program is configured for the correct com port.

A basic check that you can do is to disconnect your serial cable from the Mini and connect its Tx and Rx lines together and then type on your keyboard. You should see what you type on the keyboard reiterated in the terminal window. If not, you need to double check those comms settings.

And that's it. With some luck you now have access to the internal operating system and software of your Mini.

You can now move to the next chapter.

7.1.2.1 Forum64 (German)

Here is another similar yet slightly different way to change games directly in the Mini.

https://www.forum64.de/index.php?thread/81623-thec64-mini-modding-uart-schnittstelle-f%C3%BCr-seriellen-root-zugriff/&postID=1257297#post1257297

or search in the Forum for "thec64-mini-modding-uart-schnittstelle" (German).

7.1.3 Software Root Access

Here, I provide you with some insights on how to get root access to the Mini.

Before you start, download the VICE Emulator and install it.

- WINVICE 2.4 (for Linux-he: NO SDL VICE!)

Additionally, you will need:

- Image editing software, Photoshop or similar, e.g. Irfanview
http://irfanview.com

- A good text editor – can recommend here Notepad ++
http://notepad-plus-plus.org

- 7-zip to compress the VICE snapshots, to be found at
http://7-zip.org

Important: Setting the root password:

Connect your Mini with UART to your computer.

Now you need the root login and to set your own password. After, you can also log in without interruption on the Mini as root.

Here is what you need to do step by step:

```
setenv nand_root /dev/sda
boot
insmod /lib/modules/3.4.39/nand.ko
mount /dev/nandb /mnt
passwd
(Type in a password) [ The cursor does not move, the input is masked]
(confirm password again) [ The cursor does not move, the input is masked]
mv /mnt/etc/shadow /mnt/etc/shadow.old
cp /etc/shadow /mnt/etc
umount /mnt
Here is the entire text:
redquark # setenv nand_root /dev/sda
redquark # boot
read boot or recovery all
[48.085] sunxi flash read: offset 1000000, 11549075 bytes OK
[48.100] ready to boot
[48.103] [mmc]: MMC Device 2 not found
[48.107] [mmc]: mmc not find, so not exit
```

NAND_Uboot

Exit

NB1 : NAND_LogicExit

[48.111] Starting kernel ...

[0.991847] rtc_hw_init

(416) err: set clksrc to external losc failed! rtc time wants to be wrong

[1.001419] sunxi_rtc_gettime (34): err, losc_err_flag is 1 [1.076451] [hdmi] hdmi module init

[1.082448] ## fb init: w = 1280, h = 720, fbmode = 0

[1.099610] sunxi_rtc_gettime

(34): err, losc_err_flag is 1

[1.105737] sunxi-rtc sunxi-rtc: hctosys: unable to read the hardware clockroot = /dev/sdawait /dev/sda readywait /dev/sda readywait / dev/sda readywait /dev/sda ready

[4.953983] sd 0: 0: 0: 0: [sda] No Caching mode page present

[4.960123] sd 0: 0: 0: 0: [sda] Assuming drive cache:

/ # insmod /lib/modules/3.4.39/nand.ko

/ # mount /dev /nandb/mnt

[65.852040] EXT4-fs (nandb): could not mount as ext3 due to feature incompatibilities

[65.944133] EXT4-fs (nandb): could not mount as ext2 due to feature incompatibilities

/ # passwd Changing password for root

New password: (type in password)

Retype password: (type password again)

Password for root changed by root

/ # mv /mnt/etc/shadow /mnt/etc/shadow.old

/ # cp /etc/shadow /mnt/etc

/ # umount /mnt

/ #

Then, restart the Mini and log in with login: root and the password you set. Now you have root access to the Mini :)

Backing up NAND memory and existing games

Next, I would first make backup copies of the NAND memory and all the games on the USB stick. You never know if you will need it later or if you would need about 210MB of free space on the stick…

Since the guys from Retro Games fiddled with the mount standard, the USB stick has to be integrated a bit differently. As root you are already logged in, now enter the following:

    mount /tmp/usbdrive/sda1 /mnt

Then you copy the nand parts to the USB stick with:

    cp /dev/nand* /mnt

and now the games files:

    cp /usr/share/the64/games/*.tsg /mnt/games/
    cp /usr/share/the64/games/games/* /mnt/games/games/
    cp /usr/share/the64/games/covers/* /mnt/games/covers/
    cp /usr/share/the64/games/screens/* /mnt/games/screens/

and which joysticks are all supported copies the following txt file:

    cp /usr/share/the64/ui/data/gamecontrollerdb.txt /mnt

Then unmount the USB stick with:

    umount /mnt

Now "shut down" the Mini with

    poweroff

and disconnect the power plug again.

Now you can unplug the USB stick and plug it into your PC and copy the backed-up files for backup somewhere else.

    nanda: Linux kernel
    nandb: root filesystem, ext2 format
    nandc:? probably additional memory, contains nothing.
    gamecontrollerdb.txt
    Game files in the games directory

For the most part is to do root first and then make backups.

Extra steps for Path B

For Path B (if you want your extra games on the USB stick only), you need to do the following steps as well:

- plug the USB stick into the Mini

- power up the Mini

- log in as root

I'll now focus on the extra steps on page 7 of this forum thread: http://thec64community.online/thread/4/modding-thec64-mini?page=7

- Make the root path writable with:

    mount -o remount,rw /
    Create a new folder to mount this 2nd partition later on
    mkdir /mnt2
    Make a backup of "/etc/fstab" as follows:
    mount /tmp/usbdrive/sda1 /mnt
    cp /etc/fstab /mnt
    umount /mnt
    Edit "/etc/fstab", adding the bolded lines (I'll use "vi /etc/fstab" to make the edit.
    # <file system> <mount pt> <type> <options> <dump> <pass>
    /dev/root / ext2 rw,noauto 0 1
    /dev/sda2 /mnt2 ext4 rw,nofail 0 0
    /mnt2/usr/share/the64 /usr/share/the64 none bind,nofail 0 0
    /mnt2/var/lib/the64 /var/lib/the64 none bind,nofail 0 0
    proc /proc proc defaults 0 0
    devpts /dev/pts devpts defaults,gid=5,mode=620 0 0
    tmpfs /dev/shm tmpfs mode=0777 0 0
    tmpfs /tmp tmpfs mode=1777 0 0
    tmpfs /run tmpfs mode=0755,nosuid,nodev 0 0
    sysfs /sys sysfs defaults 0 0
    Add an "/etc/init.d" startup script to ensure the directories are mounted:
    cat >/etc/init.d/S98mountusb
    #!/bin/sh
    mount -a

```
<CTRL>-D
chmod a+x /etc/init.d/S98mountusb
```

Ok then, I guess we're done with these steps, so maybe you should now turn off the power:

```
poweroff
```

copy the contents of nandb over to your 2nd partition on the USB stick with this command:

```
dd if=/dev/nandb of=/dev/sda2
```

You've successfully backed up the NAND

SUNXI: The http://linux-sunxi.org/Retro_Games_Ltd_RGL001 site has a nice description of how to connect to the serial port and access the root filesystem on NAND. If you do this (and are willing to void your warranty and at your own risk) you can experiment with adding games and joysticks, changing the music that's playing, etc.

But this can be a bit tricky and you will lose your guarantee on the Mini.

Important directories

The emulator: /usr/bin/the64. This seems to be a combination of a VICE clone and menu/Game loader.

Game data

Game description files: /usr/share/the64/games. Each game has a <game-name.tsg> text file that contains thegame title, description in various languages, game cover and screenshots, joystick settings etc.

Game covers are in /usr/share/the64/games/covers, screenshots in /usr/share/the64/games/screens

Game code is in /usr/share/the64/games/games. Each game is a compressed VICE snapshot file but not compatible with the standard VICE 3.1 nor standard 2.4.

Joysticks are recognized if they are found in /usr/share/the64/ui/data/gamecontrollerdb.txt.

Game snapshots slots are saved in a directory per game /var/lib/the64/profile/0/saves/<gamename>.

Adding Games

The easiest way to add a game is to first load it via BASIC and then save a snapshot. You can then copy the <slot#>.vsf to the games directory as /usr/share/the64/games/games/<gamename>.vsf.gz[and the screenshot <slot#>.png to /usr/share/the64/games/games/<gamename>-01.png. Then you have to create a /usr/share/the64/games/<gamename>.tgs file as well, taking an existing one as example.

Adding Joysticks

The most important thing is the joystick settings. However, the line (or 2 lines in 2 joystick games) is always structured as follows:

J1 (*) / 2 (*): JU, JD, JL, JR, LEFT trigger, RIGHT trigger, LEFT shift pad, right shift pad, Y, B, A, back (= BACK / SELECT button), X

At each position, you always have to fill in what the joystick buttons should do and what keys on the Mini keyboard they press.

Shortcuts are:

- JF = JOYSTICK FIRE / FIRE KEY

- F1 ... F8 = F-keys

- RS = RUNSTOP

- SP = SPACE / SPACEBAR

- EN = ENTER / RETURN

- or letters / numbers

The first 4 directional abbreviations (JU, JD, JL, JR) can also be lettered, for example, to play old games that support only keys for control. The best example is probably Frogger ;) A joystick line could look like this:

J: 2 * : W, S, A, D, Y, N „, F „ S, F1, JF

- W, S, A, D on the Dpad

- Y, N on the trigger's buttons L / R

- F on Y button

- S again on A button

- F1 on Back or Select buttons

- FIRE on X button

keys that are not used do not have to be mapped either, but the row must always have the 13-variable size after the colon, separated by commas.

To add e.g. the much-coveted Speedlink Pro, add the following line to /usr/share/the64/ui/data/gamecontrollerdb.txt:

Code:

```
030000000b0400003365000000010000,Speed-Link
Competition Pro,a:b1,b:b5,x:b6,y:b7,back:b3,s
tart:b2,lefttrigger:b0,righttrigger:b4,leftx:
a0,lefty:a1,platform:Linux,
```

The 32-digit number is what identifies the joystick and is based on how the joystick identifies itself on USB including the HID version. E.g. my Speedlink reports itself (from dmesg) as:

Code:

```
generic-USB 0003:040B:6533.0002: input: USB
HID v1.00 Joystick [A SPEED-LINK Competition
Pro]
```

To get the number reverse the (2-byte) order of each of the first 3 numbers, add four 0's after each number and add the reverse-order HID version number plus four 0's. Then, you have to experiment with the button (b0..x) and axis (a0..ax) assignment. For the Speedlink, I used the left fire button as fire, the right fire button as the 'load' button (left small red button on the original joystick) and the two triangular buttons as 'menu' and 'save'.

If you don't want to modify the NAND filesystem you can also copy it to an USB drive and experiment with that. This is much safer as you run less risk of breaking the system:

Create two partitions on the USB stick, the first one a FAT that you'll use for storing whatever THEC64-drive8.d64 you use. The second one should be an ext4 partition.

Insert the USB stick into the Mini USB slot and switch the Mini on.

At the command prompt copy the root filesystem to it: Assuming your ext4 USB partition is sda2 the command is dd if=/dev/nandb of=/dev/sda2.

Use the trick from the Sunxi page to use this as root filesystem, in u-boot enter (setenv NAND_root /dev/sda2). Note you have this at every reboot, the saveenv command doesn't work.

More to read can be found here: http://thec64community.online/ thread/4/modding-thec64-mini

7.1.3.1 FEL Mode

See also: 4.3 Pin assignment & buttons

Here's a tip: There is a remote button that will start FEL mode which is located underneath the device manufacturer's sticker. This allows you to enter FEL without disassembling the case.

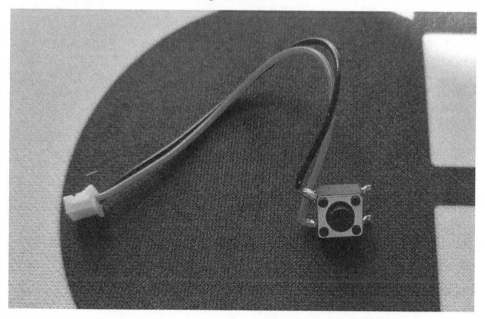

The hole is under the first 0 from RGL001 (see photo).

FEL is a low-level subroutine that is used for initial programming and recovery of devices using USB and is contained in the BootROM on Allwinner devices.

The device needs to be attached to a host PC by an USB cable, which is connected to a port where the Sunxi device will be present as slave in device mode.

More to read can be found here: http://linux-sunxi.org/FEL

7.1.4 Adding games to the carousel and changing the music

Assuming you already have added a UART connector to the Mini and established a connection, this is the preparation you have to do first:

Generate a folder called "gamesnew" on your USB-stick. In this folder generate the folders "covers", "screens" and "games".

For each game you want to use, all filenames have to be exactly the same beside the extension.

In "covers" you put a picture of the cover in .png 122x175 Pixel and 32Bit.

In "screens" you put a picture of the start screen in "gamename-00.png" and a screenshot of the game in "gamename-01.png". 320x200 in 24Bit.

In "games" you put the game as a Vice Snapshot-File, renamed to "gamename.vsf.gz" packed with gzip http://gnuwin32.sourceforge.net/packages/gzip.htm.

And in the main folder you lay the .tsg file according to the game as "gamename.tsg".

Now you can start:

1) Copy the folder "gamesnew" to the root of your USB stick. Copy only the tsg files you want to add and note that the carousel supports only 100 "tsg" files.

2) Insert your stick in the Mini and turn it on.

3) Wait for the login request and insert your password.

4) Then launch these commands:

mount /tmp/usbdrive/sda1 /mnt <<< This mount the USB-stick content to /mnt
ls /mnt <<< This will display the files on the stick
mount -o remount, rw / <<< This make the Mini folder writable
cp /mnt/gamesnew/*tsg /usr/share/the64/games <<< Copy all .tsg files to the Mini
cp /mnt/gamesnew/covers/* /usr/share/the64/games/covers <<< Copy all covers
cp /mnt/gamesnew/games/* /usr/share/the64/games/games <<< Copy all games
cp /mnt/gamesnew/screens/* /usr/share/the64/games/screens <<< Copy all screen files
5) Verify you have no more than 100 tsg files. Then launch:
ls /usr/share/the64/games <<< Display the tsg files
6) If you have more than 100 you can rename some to hide them from the carousel with:
mv /usr/share/the64/games/NAME-OF-GAME.tsg /usr/share/the64/games/NAME-OF-GAME.old
If you want to change the carousel music read this. Else go to 7)
For this you have to swap the "menu.wav" file. That wav file must be MONO, 22050 Hz, 16bit. Rename the old .wav to .old

mv /usr/share/the64/ui/sounds/menu.wav /usr/share/the64/ui/sounds/menu.old

cp /mnt/NEW.wav /usr/share/the64/ui/sounds <<< Copy "NEW.wav" from USB-stick to internal folder

Rename "NEW.wav" to "menu.wav" (watch Capital letters)

mv /usr/share/the64/ui/sounds/ocean.wav /usr/share/the64/ui/sounds/menu.wav

7) To finish, launch:

mount -o remount, ro / <<< Restore Mini folders back to "readonly"

umount /mnt <<< Unmount the stick

poweroff <<< Power the Mini off

8) Wait for the power to be turned off, unplug the stick and play your new games.

A "short" checklist

- GAME.tsg (in "games.new/") GAME

- GAME-cover.png (in "games.new/covers/")

- GAME-00.png, GAME-01.png (in "games.new/screens/")

- GAME.vsf.gz (in "games.new/games/")

If you have all these together, then you can plug the USB stick with the files to the Mini and setup the serial and connection with the UART adapter and click on Putty. After that, you just have to copy your files to the Mini.

Log in first as root.
Mount the USB stick:
mount /tmp/usbdrive/sda1 /mnt

- The root drive is mounted as READ-ONLY, you have to change it to be able to write on it:

mount -o remount, rw /

- Then copy your files from your stick to the root drive:

(-i causes it to ask beforehand if it should overwrite a file, sometimes wanted or not)

(-f, for example, causes it to overwrite without prompting)

(-r would be directory with Copy subdirectories but I prefer to have a little more control and do it one by one.)

(Type only cp (copy command) will show a help text of what options you can use.)

```
cp -i /mnt/games.new/*.tsg /usr/share/the64/games/
cp -i /mnt/games.new/covers/* /usr/share/the64/games/covers/
cp -i /mnt/games.new/games/* /usr/share/the64/games/games/
cp - i /mnt/games.new/screens/* /usr/share/the64/games/
screens/
After copying, put the root drive back in READ-ONLY state:
mount -o remount, ro /
And unmount the USB stick with:
umount /mnt
```

Lastly, upon turning off the power, shut down the Mini and unplug the power plug again.

Now you can screw the Mini back together (I have my own that is always open in the meantime), Now you can turn on the Mini, switch on your TV and hopefully enjoy one (or more) new game(s) on it.

I wish you a lot of fun and success.

7.1.5 Replacing the kernal and 1541 DOS ROM

mike251Mike251 wrote this text on the64community.online. If you like to comment or mail him, please visit this page: http://thec64community. online/thread/80/replacing-stock-c64-kernal-1541

Hello again, Modders!

Ok, so you've taken the leap and added the UART to your Mini and now you are eager to make those programs in your D64 image load quicker, here's how you go about doing that.

First thing I'll say is I am not responsible for any damage you do to your Mini and as with any modification of this type there is always a chance that you could break it.

Second is that this is really a combination of a few threads that I've seen when cruising around looking for Mini modding info. I just thought I'd try and tie it all up in to one post.

So on to it, shall we.

What you will need:

- PuTTY (as per my post Adding a UART) https://www.chiark.greenend. org.uk/~sgtatham/putty/latest.html

- JiffyDOS C64 Kernal Image http://store.go4retro.com/ jiffydos-64-kernal-rom-overlay-image/

- JiffyDOS 1541-II DOS ROM Image http://store.go4retro.com/ jiffydos-1541-dos-rom-overlay-image/

- USB memory stick.

Let's get started!

Partition your USB memory stick so that it has two partitions, each one should be formatted as FAT32

Copy your JiffyDOS Kernal and 1541-II ROM images to the SECOND partition. For the sake of this example, let's assume the filenames for your images are JiffyDOS_C64.bin and JiffyDOS_1541-II.bin. Yes, the Mini version of VICE is using the 1541-II disk drive emulation.

Plug in your USB to TTL adaptor and launch PuTTY. Settings should look something like this

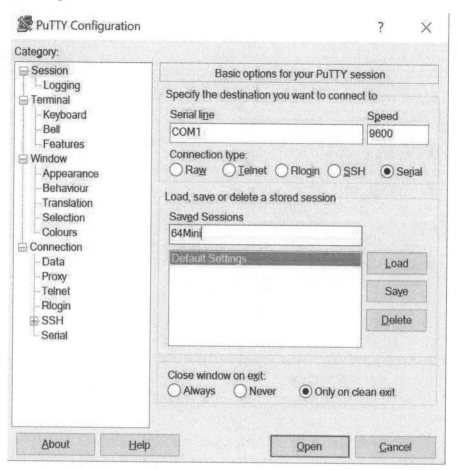

Follow the guide here that outlines the method required to change the password for the 'root' account.

So, now you should have set a password for the root account and be logged in. You can start snooping around!

Have a look at this Linux Quick Guide for some examples of how to list a directory, change directory, etc.

Folders of interest are:

/usr/bin contains the executable 'the64' which has already been mentioned appears to be a customized version of VICE containing the Game carousel

/usr/lib/vice contains the standard VICE folders C64, DRIVES, PRINTER and fonts

If you want to have some peace and quiet while you are exploring the system you can terminal vice by typing ps and press enter. This will show a list of process numbers and what they are. Have a look for the process number associated with the 'the64' process. Mine shows up as 760, so the command would be kill -9 760

The commands to get JiffyDOS on your 64Mini are:

```
cd / #start at top level of folder structure
mount -o remount, rw / #set filesystem to r/w
mount /dev/sda2 /mnt #mount second partition of USB flash drive
cd /usr/lib/vice/C64 #vice folder containing C64 Kernal, etc
mv Kernal Kernal.bak #backup the stock Kernal
cp /mnt/JiffyDOS_C64.bin Kernal #copy new Kernal from USB and
rename it Kernal
chmod 644 Kernal #give it the same file permissions as the original
has
cd /usr/lib/vice/DRIVES #change to vice drive ROM folder
mv d1541-II d1541-II.bak #backup stock 1541 drive ROM
cp /mnt/JiffyDOS_1541-II.bin d1541-II #copy JiffyDOS drive ROM
from USB and rename it
chmod 644 d1541-II #give it the same file permissions the original
has
```

You do not type the # symbol or my comments after it, that's just there so you know why you have typed what you did. Don't forget to press enter after every command.

Once you're done, type reboot and hit enter. The Mini will restart and you should hopefully have a working Mini with JiffyDOS.

More for you to read can be found here: http://thec64community. online/thread/80/replacing-stock-c64-kernal-1541

7.1.6 U-Boot trick

This instruction that https://www.linuxjournal.com/content/handy-u-boot-trick provided helps to create a system to develop and deploy bare-metal programs and Kernal images quickly. You may want to look at u-boot-v2 "Barebox". This code modification is to compile the U-Boot with an elaborate boot sequence that could be tailored with the least modifications. Try out some fancy scripts and check or update firmware over LAN.

For any questions or suggestions, you can write to bharath@lohray.com.

7.1.7 Source code

This text is from the official THEC64.com webpage!

Open Source code in THEC64 Mini?

Yes, there is some. You may obtain the corresponding open source code from us for a period of three years after our last shipment of this product, by sending a money order or cheque for 5GBP to: GPL Compliance Division, Retro Games Ltd. Suite 112, Crystal House, New Bedford Road, Luton, England. LU1 1HS. Please write "source for <firmware version number>" in the memo line of your payment.

7.2 Faster CPU

Question: Can the whole system or the onboard CPU be accelerated to play e.g. SuperCPU-Games?

Answer: Unfortunately, this is not possible. The timing of the hardware makes this impossible and it wasn't considered in the planning because this is too special of a case for too few games.

Also, the SuperCPU is not just a quicker CPU. It's much more than that and is a complex additional hardware.

More about that can be read here: http://supercpu.cbm8bit.com/

8 Disks, images & formats

In these pages you will find a lot of information on disk formats:

http://www.baltissen.org/newhtm/diskimag.htm

https://ist.uwaterloo.ca/~schepers/formats.html

https://www.c64-wiki.de/wiki/disk-image

8.1 Bootloader

A Bootloader automatically loads all included parts of a program.

So far, all programs that have loaded additional program data via a Bootloader have worked properly.

Please do not confuse this with the second next coming chapter 8.3 Multi-disk games. That is another matter.

If anyone has other experiences with this, please write to me and I will correct or extend this paragraph.

8.2 How to use D81/D82

This describes how to use D81 and D82 files on the Mini.

Tip: I mostly use a D82 image which has more space and allows you to fit about 1mb of games on it.

Only for firmware older than 1.1.0: Rename the D81/D82 image you created for example, with DirMaster to THEC64-drive8.d64 and save it in the root directory of your USB stick and plug it into the Mini.

Firmware 1.1.0 and higher: Rename the D81/ D82 image you created with DirMaster so that it has the file extension .d64 then save it on your USB stick and then insert into the Mini. Open a game from the carousel (Alleykat because it's the first to find and have a built-in Fastloader)

Exit Alleykat

Start BASIC

If you like, type LOAD"*",8,1 (without the return key)

Make the save state now!

So for the next time you start up the machine, just jump to this BASIC save state and you won't need to jump into a carousel game in order to get the Fastloader and D81 image support.

If the Fastloader has been enabled in BASIC, but you want to turn the Fastloader off, e.g. to load a game which has its own Fastloader which isn't compatible with the inbuilt one, then, a quick way to disable the Fastloader (rather than turn the system off and on again) is to load Armalyte (which has no Fastloader) again and exit it. Then, jump back to BASIC.

TIP: Some programs/games might not work in a D82. If that is the case, use D64 or D81. You just simply have to try it out.

8.2.1 CBM 1581 Copy

This is for the nerds who still have D81 disks and want to save them.

Here you will find the Version 0.54 of the CBM 1581 floppy disk copy util for DOS. It should be able to import or export a CBM 1581 disk on a PC based 3.5" floppy drive and disk controller.

More to read is here: http://d81.de/

8.3 Multi-disk games

See also: 10.2 More games

8.3.1 Playing games that span multiple disks (1.2.0)

If you have upgraded to firmware V1.1.4 (highly recommended!), then you can use this new disk-swapping workaround which you also should use with V1.2.0:

You can use Multidisks by giving both images the same name. With this, you have the same savestate for one game. You have to make folders then (ex. "Side A") to seperate the files.

I already tried it and it works. But it's a hassle if you have many sides and you have to copy in every folder the same cjm file.*

You have the game folder. Then, there must be a new folder per side. The game must have the same name in every folder. If you have to change the disk, save the game. Then, select the needed side and load the savestate you did before.

8.3.2 Play multi-disk games (Firmware older than 1.1.0)

There are some limitations to the existing method of loading programs from an USB memory stick:

For C64 programs that need a joystick, only joystick port 2 is currently usable. This will be improved with our advanced loader, coming in a future firmware update. Our apologies if this causes a short delay before you can use your favourite program correctly.

At present, THEC64 Mini can only load .d64 files using the current method. This will change when the advanced loader is released!

Joystick-buttons other than the menu-button and the two main fire buttons currently have no functionality in programs loaded from an USB memory stick. Again, this will change when the advanced loader is released.

Due to licensing requirements, we cannot offer advice as to which programs currently work using this method and which ones do not.

All the supplied games are pre-configured to work correctly on Mini. The advanced loader will significantly increase the number of programs that work and we are planning to get this firmware upgrade ready for release as soon as possible.

Multi-Disk-Games

Provided that the first disk of a Multi-Disk-Program works correctly, you can swap disks on the Mini at the required moment. For a two-disk program, the current procedure is as follows:

• When you are asked to change or flip disks in the program, press the MENU button on the joystick and save your current position in one of the four slots available to BASIC

• Exit to the carousel and then remove the USB memory stick from the Mini

• (Only firmware older 1.1.0) Insert the USB memory stick into a computer and rename THEC64-drive8.d64 to something else memorable – let's say MYDISK1.d64

• (Only firmware older 1.1.0) Copy the second disk image file to the USB stick and name it THEC64-drive8.d64

• (Only firmware older 1.1.0) Pop the USB stick back into the Mini, ensuring you're still on the carousel screen

• Launch BASIC from the carousel

• Press the MENU button on the joystick and load the position you saved earlier from one of the slots on the Mini

- Follow any on-screen instructions from your program regarding what to do next.

- If at some point the program needs the first disk again, follow the above instructions from step 1

- (Only firmware older 1.1.0) this time rename THEC64-drive8.d64 on the memory stick to something else (e.g. MYDISK2.d64), then rename the other disk image file to THEC64-drive8.d64).

This is significantly improved with our advanced loader (firmware newer as 1.1.0) as with all other aspects of loading programs.

8.3.3 Make you own multi-disk images

By making your own multi-disk images for the Mini, you can choose from several games at one Menu:

- Download FIBR (This is a small menu program that you should start first on every disk)

- Download DirMaster, install and run it

- Select: Disk / New / D82

- Drag the FIBR.PRG, into the new disk, so that it's always the first file on the disk

- Take the games .prg files and drag them into the disk

- Save the disk and change the file extension from. d82 to .d64

- (Only necessary for firmware older 1.1.0) Rename the file to THEC64-drive8.d64

- Copy the file on an USB stick and Plug it into the Mini

- Turn the Mini on and load e.g. AlleyKat or Avenger

- Hint! Not all games in the carousel activate the Fastloader support (read more about it in 3.6 Fastloaders)

- Press the Menu button on the joystick

- Start BASIC

- Type LOAD"*",8,1 and the press Enter button

- Type: RUN and press the Enter button

- Use the joystick to select a game and press fire to load it

- Have Fun!

8.3.4 Multi-load concept from tape

You will find on this webpage a method of splitting a game into multiple parts to get around memory constraints, particularly on tape-based formats such as the ZX Spectrum and Commodore 64. (Link at the bottom!)

COMMODORE 64 - CASSETTE

Position the cassette in your Commodore recorder with the printed side upwards and make sure that it is rewound to the beginning.

Ensure that all the leads are connected.

Press the SHIFT key and the RUN/STOP key simultaneously.

Follow the screen instruction - PRESS PLAY ON TAPE.

This program will then load automatically.

For C128 loading type GO 64 (RETURN), then follow C64 instruction.

PLEASE NOTE: This game loads in a number of parts.

Depending on the route you take, the loading may not be sequential on the tape. To assist you, an on-screen message will tell you which file it is searching for and which file it is currently reading. The list below illustrates the sequential order that these parts appear on the tape. You may need to fast forward or rewind the tape in order to find the appropriate section. It is advisable to reset the tape-counter at the start of the tape and then make a note of the tape-counter number as each file is found.

1. PICTURE 4 GAME MID 7 ESCAPE 2. INTRO 5 GAME BOT 8 THE END 3. GAME TOP 6 BAPTIZED

NOTE: SIDE B is identical to SIDE A.

DISK Select 64 mode.

Turn on the disk drive, insert the program into the drive with the label facing upwards.

Type LOAD"*",8,1 (RETURN); the introductory screen will appear and the program will then load automatically.

More Info you will get if you follow the link: https://www.giantbomb.com/multi-load/3015-7586/

8.4 Converting file formats

Do you still have programs or games in a file format that the Mini does not support? No problem!

With the program DirMaster it is possible to import the file in the foreign format and save it as another format (D64).

Or, it is also possible with the older 64Copy which can convert formats directly.

D64 files are disk images for the C64 and PRG files can be loaded inside this disk file image.

DirMaster copies a PRG file from the PC into a D64 file. Then it can be loaded and run in the Mini.

D64 files can also contain other file formats like SEQ and RND.

This way you can use even .tap or .t64.

8.5 Disk image formats

The single sided 5¼" Disk-Formats for the Floppy 1541 also apply for the VC-1540, 1551, 1570 and 1571.

5¼ Inch Disks:

- D64 for Floppy 1541, 1551, 1571, ect. - Single sided
- D71 Floppy 1571 Double sided
- D80 Floppy 8050 Single sided
- D82 Floppy 8250
- P64 Floppy 1541
- FDI Floppy 1541

3½ Inch Disks:

- D81 Floppy 1581
- G64 Single sided "G41"
- D2M/D4M Floppy CMD FD-2000/FD-4000

For Disks in different sizes:

- X64

Other Commodore File formats:

- 64x PC64/DOS ROM File
- ARC Compressed ARChive
- ARK ARKive Containers
- BIN Binary Raw Files - ROM-Dumps
- C64 PC64 saved-session File
- C64 PCLINK Container File
- CIS Packed File
- CRT Expansionsport-Modul-Image
- CVT Archiv-Format for GEOS-VLIR-Files/Programs
- DMP DC2N TAP RAW Format
- F64 A companion File to certain D64's
- FRZ C64s saved-session FRoZen Files
- L64 64LAN Container File
- LBR LiBRary Containers, C64 version only
- LHA/LZH/LZS LHArc compressed Files
- LNX LyNX Container Files
- N64 64NET Container File
- NBZ/NIB MNIB-1541-RAW Format
- P00 Program File incl. original File name
- P01 C64 File incl. original File name
- PCV PCVIC VIC-20 emulator saved-session File
- PRG Program File
- PRW Program File format
- REL RELative File layout
- ROM Dump File
- S00/U00/R00 PC64 emulator Container Files
- S20 Phau Zeh VIC-20 emulator saved-session File

- SDA Self-Dissolving compressed Archive
- SEQ Program File format
- SFX SelF-eXtracting LHA/LZH compressed File
- SID/PSID Various SIDPlay / PlaySID Formats
- SPY SPYne Containers
- T64 Container for PRG
- T64 Tape Containers for C64
- TAP Datasette (Cassette) -Image
- TAP Raw C64 Cassette TAPE Image
- VSF VICE Snapshot-Images
- VSF Vice Snapshot File, saved-session File
- WAR/WR3 WRAptor Compressed Files
- WAV RIFF Audio File
- X64 X64 and VICE Emulator Image File
- Z64 ZIP64 Zipcode Files
- ZIP PKZip Compressed Files

8.5.1 M2I

M2I is something like an image format created for the MMC2IEC. It has no size limit and has a save function. Any number of files of d64 images can be stored in it so that multidisk/reload programs or individual disks function without problems.

In Forum64 there is a collective thread for M2I where you can also find converted games. https://www.forum64.de/index. php?thread/19522-m2i-sammelthread/

More for you to read on this webpage: https://www.c64-wiki.de/wiki/ sd2iec_(Firmware)

8.5.1.1 M2I games

See also: 10 Games & downloads

This is an old website with 328 C64 games in M2i format. http://www. creepitz.de/downloads/m2i/

8.5.2 Decoding the F64 filetype

This page is for all who are interested in understanding how the F64 Format works.

More for you to read on this webpage: http://ist.uwaterloo.ca/~schepers/ F64.html

9 Tips & tricks

9.1 Slow directory listing

When loading the file inventory of a disk the old-fashioned way and LIST it, hold down CTRL to slowly browse through the list until you see what you want. Then press STOP.

9.2 Turning off the Mini

Usually, when a Mini is USB powered it switches back on automatically and continues after you switch it off.

Just press and hold the button for a few seconds to turn it off completely.

Or, switch the USB power off by switching off the power supply or by pulling the cable.

9.3 Starting / playing a game

TIP: To start a game and to be able to use all buttons of the joystick without interference, you should disable the virtual keyboard and only switch it back on when necessary.

9.4 Keyboard buffer

Once you have typed LOAD"$",8 and loaded the directory, in the meantime you can enter LIST and press the RETURN button. A small buffer remembers these entries and executes LIST directly after the directory has been fully loaded.

For example, this works with RUN as well.

9.5 Use save games as highscore table.

Many games on the C64 do not save the highscores on disk. With save states you can easily reserve your high-scores. This way, you can restore the game the next time you play, keeping the scores intact and you can start over again to beat your own record.

Also, don't forget to take a picture of your high-scores and submit them to online High-Scores Archives.

10 Games & downloads

See also: 8.5.1.1 M2I games, 5.2.2 4-player mode, 3.4
Disk management, 9.3 Starting / playing a game

10.1 Sam's Journey

You can also play the hit platformer "Sam's Journey" by "Knights of Bytes" on your THEC64 Mini (PAL).

This really great game has been mentioned again and again in connection with the Mini. In that respect, I can resolve and explain a few things here.

There have been conversations between Retro Games Ltd. and Knights of Bytes in 2016. However, at the time the game was not yet finished and the intended device was still called THE64. Yet, a signed contract never came about.

Sam's Journey was unfortunately not playable on the Mini at that time. The reason for this was the lack of support for firmware for games that include multiple disk images or a cartridge image. Since Knight for Bytes wanted to give the player a really great gaming experience, the deal did not push through.

The Digital Download Edition is available at Protovision or itch.io and includes four D64 image files. You should proceed with these files exactly as described in 8.3 Multi-disk games.

If you prefer to hold something in your hands, you can order the game on real disks or as a cartridge in a nice box with a printed manual and all kinds of gimmicks at Protovision. Access to downloads is also included.

https://www.knightsofbytes.games/samsjourney

https://www.protovision.games/games/sams_journey.php?language=en

10.1.1 Steel Ranger

From the same developer, here is a highly modern game that runs really nice on the Mini.

10.2 More games

See also: 3.2.1 DirMaster, 8.3 Multi-disk games

Question: Will there be more games included? If so, which ones?

Retro Games: Retro Games is in constant discussion with games' rights owners and they do anticipate further games be added to current and future versions of THEC64 range. However, they can't at this time confirm on specific titles other than to say it's almost certain to happen.

Question: What if you get offered games to use for free. Will you include them?

Retro Games: Retro Games has been already offered free games and they are considering all ways to make these available to both current and future users of THEC64 range.

10.2.1 Organism

Amazing news! Our friends over at Psytronik have released a new game and that has a specific THEC64 Mini version you can buy that goes straight on an USB stick to use with your Mini!

https://psytronik.itch.io/organism-c64

10.2.2 Legend of Atlantis

Here's more, keep them coming!

http://www.psytronik.net/newsite/index.php/c64

https://psytronik.itch.io/legend-of-atlantis

10.3 Downloads

10.3.1 C64 Forever

To experience and relive this unique computer, Cloanto has introduced C64 Forever. It's the official CBM 8-bit preservation, emulation and support package. https://www.c64forever.com/

With an intuitive player interface, supported by a built-in database of more than 5,000 games, it supports RP9 format, allowing advanced title authoring and easy cross-platform playback.

RP9 (from RetroPlatform) is a packaging format largely compatible with the format endorsed by the W3C for web applications.

RP9 file is a ZIP archive (zip renamed to rp9) containing one or more disk-image files (e.g. ADF, D64, etc.) and an XML manifest (rp9-manifest.xml, as per RP9 XML Schema).

You can easily extract the well know formats like .d64 out of an RP9-File by renaming it from .rp9 to .zip. Now it's a usual ZIP-Archive -File which you even can open with Windows Explorer.

10.3.2 64er.de

Here you will find Emulators - Games - SIDs - Downloads - Forum - Support: http://www.64er.de/

10.3.3 File manager overview (German)

See also: 10 Games & downloads

Here you will find a nice overview of file managers suitable for the C64 and the Mini.

https://www.c64-wiki.de/wiki/Dateinavigator

10.3.4 C64 Online (German)

Just browse through here. There is a lot to discover: https://c64-online.com/?page_id=109

10.3.5 Gamesbase64

See also: 12.4.1 High Voltage SID Collection

GameBase64 is the most comprehensive database for C64 games: http://www.gamebase64.com/

There are no real playable games in this database. It includes only descriptions. To play the games, you have to own them. So far there are over 25000 entries in the database. It is constantly updated and maintained by fans from all over the world.

There is also an offline version of GameBase64 that can be downloaded for free. The Frontend exists for Windows and for Linux and Mac OS X as "jGameBase". The games can then be run directly in an emulator.

The GameBase64 is suitable for all emulators. Additional emulators can be configured by the user. Music from the game entries can be played in SID players via a link to the High Voltage SID Collection.

10.3.5.1 Gamebase64 front end

Here you get the best front end out there from the most complete game collection database there is for the C64: http://www.gamebase64.com/gamebase.php

10.3.5.2 Gamebase64 projects

On this site you can find information about some Commodore 64 related projects that are mostly for the GameBase Frontend: https://sites.google.com/site/kc64projects/

Introbase64: A GameBase collection of all intros can be found at http://intros.c64.org. Currently, the collection has over 9000 entries.

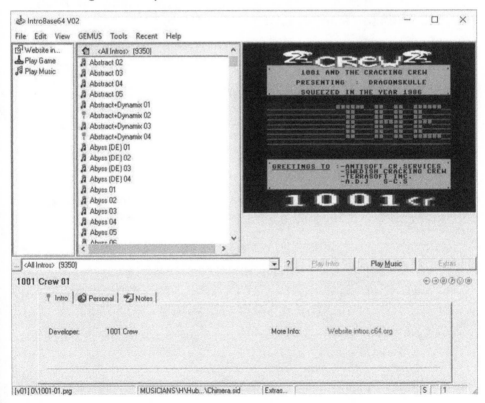

Intros reorganizer: A script that reorganizes the intros package is being offered at http://intros.c64.org for easy browsing with a 1541 Ultimate cartridge.

gb64manual: The manual covering the installation and usage of the GameBase64 Collection. The manual can be read online and downloaded for printing your own booklet.

gbxfer: A set of scripts that integrates OpenCBM in the GameBase Frontend. With OpenCBM, C64 file archives (like D64 files) can be written to real floppies using a Windows PC and a connected Commodore floppy drive. http://opencbm.sourceforge.net/

GBXfer adds this feature to GameBase. First, select the game you want to play, then right click on the Play-Game-Button and choose "Transfer to real floppy". The selected game will automatically be transferred to a real 5.25" floppy to allow the game to be played on real hardware.

appsntoolsbase64: A GameBase collection containing all kinds of Commodore 64 software except games and demos.

Games and demos are already covered in The GameBase Collection and DemoBase C64. APPSnTOOLSbase64 is the collection of Commodore 64 software for the serious Commodore user!

10.4 RGCD games

RGCD (Retro Gamer CD) started as a retro-gaming, CD-based discmag first published in 2006. http://www.rgcd.co.uk/

Since 2009, RGCD has evolved into a game development team and retro publisher, concentrating on the Atari STE, PC and C64 platforms.

RGCD.DEV is a game development label for modern (i.e. non-retro) platforms.

10.4.1 Contact page

http://www.rgcd.co.uk/p/contact.html

10.5 High score

On this page you can upload your high scores and compare it with others.

There are also prices to win! :) http://www.highscore.com/

10.6 4-joystick games

See also: 5.2.2 4-player mode

Currently the feature of playing with more than 2 players at the same time is not supported. However, it is highly probable to come in future firmware.

10.6.1 Protovision (German)

On this Webpage you will find several games playable with 4 or more joysticks/players.

More to read is on the Webpage: http://www.protovision-online.de/hardw/4_player.php?language=de

10.6.2 Games that weren't

On this Webpage you will find the game Octron which can be played with up to 8 players.

More to read is on the webpage: http://www.gamesthatwerent.com/gtw64/octron/

10.7 6 hidden games?

Even though the Mini joystick looks much alike the DTV, it isn't the same. It was specially developed for the Mini.

But for those who do have the DTV, here is a little hidden Feature. The DTV has six hidden games you can play if you follow these easy steps:

- Start the DTV
- At the black and white startup screen wiggle the joystick rapidly left and right.
- A C64 Bootscreen appears already with a list of programs.
- The first brings you back to BASIC, the other 6 are games :-)

Here is an informative video showing how it's done: https://www.youtube. com/watch?v=uDwsAOaOnJU

11 Demoscene

Demos are computer-generated short films calculated in real time. They always show what kind of graphic and sound effects can be extracted from the current computer hardware, even when the music is created by one-self or on the computer.

For such demos, demosceners usually work in teams, as these demos are usually very complex and require a lot of skill in different disciplines. Graphic designers, musicians and programmers are necessary to create an executable program from all elements. The demo then runs as an independent program.

Just take a look at some of these demos and let yourself be in awe of what this little computer is capable of. These demos are what the creators of the C64 have not ever come across of in their wildest dreams.

11.1 Demos

These links lead to some favourite sites on the demo scene. There you will find old as well as the latest demos.

11.1.1 pouet.net

This is a page with news about demos, demo parties, new demos and much more that is not only for the C64.

Have a look and enjoy. http://www.pouet.net/prodlist.php

11.1.2 The best demos

Through this link you will open up a Google search that shows the very best Commodore 64 Demos.

WATCH THEM AND BE AMAZED. Search for "Best c64 demos"

11.2 High resolution graphics / NUFLI, IFLI & (A)FLI

Time after time, the scene was made surprising by features or effects, programming tricks and similar things to get the most out of the 64's hardware. A few years ago, a technique was invented that has been further developed until today in order to push the graphics of the 64 even further, e.g. to display more colors than what was actually intended. Check out the following chapters to see what has been done here.

A good first step into the topic can be found here: https://www.c64-wiki.de/wiki/FLI

11.2.1 FLI

FLI (**F**lexible **L**ine **I**nterpretation) is a technique to influence the operation of the graphics chip VIC on the C64, e.g. to change the possible colors within a tile.

More you can read here (German): https://www.c64-wiki.de/wiki/FLI

Search for Le Parc, a puzzle completely in FLI.

11.2.1.2 AFLI

AFLI (**A**dvanced **F**lexible **L**ine **I**nterpretation) is a variant of FLI. It is FLI in hires mode, which is why it is also called hires FLI.

https://www.c64-wiki.de/wiki/FLI#Hires-FLI_.28AFLI.29

11.2.1.2.1 AFLI-specs

Here you will find an explanation of what exactly FLI is, how it works and under what specifications.

http://www.antimon.org/dl/c64/code/afli.txt

11.2.1.2.2 AFLI-Editor

These are very nice tools to manipulate AFLI-Files.

https://csdb.dk/release/?id=158848

https://csdb.dk/release/?id=4388

11.2.1.3 IFLI

IFLI (**I**nterlace **FLI**) is the name for a software-driven graphics mode.

An IFLI image is displayed with a resolution of 320×200 by switching between two frames between two FLI images with 160×200. The second image is shifted to the right by half a pixel. This results in a strong flickering of the image which can be mitigated by a skillful processing of the graphics (colors with similar brightness are combined).

You can read more with following the link: https://www.c64-wiki.de/wiki/IFLI

11.2.1.4 FLI Editor

Here you can find a number of different FLI editors.

https://csdb.dk/forums/index.php?roomid=13&topicid=31731

11.2.2 NUFLI

NUFLI (**N**ew **U**nderlayed **F**lexible **L**ine **I**nterpretation) is a high-resolution and flicker-free graphic format with 320×200 pixels. In contrast to the standard hires format, there are up to 3 colors in an 8×2 are possible instead of the previous 2 colors in 8×8.

This graphics format was developed by Crest in 2009 and offers an alternative to the flickering interlace modes.

https://www.c64-wiki.de/wiki/NUFLI

11.2.2.1 NUFLI Editor

With this editor you can work on FLI Files.

Programmed by Crest, the inventor of NUFLI.

https://csdb.dk/release/?id=95473

11.2.2.2 NUFLI picture gallery

Zeldin's Gallery

These are Zeldin's 29 different C64 graphic efforts. The thumbnails are sorted by date of its making.

Click on the thumbnail on the page below to show the graphic in original C64 size including borders (384*272 pixels).

https://www.cascade64.de/csc_graphics.php?ID=142

A mouse-over symbol next to the monitor will show more info about the selected graphic.

On the bottom of the page you will find more information about the C64 graphic formats being used.

12 Internet links

Here you will find an extensive collection of many helpful and interesting links on the Internet.

12.1 Just cool pages

12.1.1 C64 web browser

See also: 4.9 Network / LAN WiFi FTP

Good to know: This web browser is called Hyperlink 2.5e. It works fine with the Commodore 64 and the follow-up, the Commodore 128. Unfortunately, because of the impossibility for the Mini to connect through ethernet, it will not really work.

But supposedly it will display JPG, GIF and TIFF images as well as standard HTML 1.0 forms and colors.

More to read and samples to see is on the webpage: http://www.ar-mory.com/~spectre/cwi/hl/

12.1.2 C64 themed webpage

Just take a look at this wonderfully themed page: http://www.retro-brothers.com/

12.1.3 Mini C64 in LEGO

Chris McVeigh is a passionate LEGO Constructor and Photographer.

He builds a nice C64 LEGO Version, which you can buy and build by yourself.

https://powerpig.ecwid.com/#!/PREORDER-%E2%80%93-
My-First-Computer-Adore-Edition-3-0/p/88336909/
category=15326690

Here is the build of the first version by Chris: https://8bitrechner.wordpress.
com/2015/04/11/lego-c64/

12.1.4 C64 running web server

Have a look at this C64 web server here: http://oldservers.ddns.net/index.
html

It runs off a standard C64 with RRNet ethernet and Contiki software. Pretty
good for a 35-year-old machine.

12.1.5 C64 Web.com

Forget simple web browsing. Using Contiki, you can even turn your Commodore 64 into a web server as well. The Commodore 64 Web V2.1 site claims to run on a 1982 Commodore 64.

http://c64web.com/

12.1.6 64er Online (German)

On this official website all issues of the legendary "64'er Magazine" are available for download as PDF files. The magazines are a must read.

http://www.64er-online.de/museum/64er_magazin.html

The first issue of the 64'er Magazine appeared in 1984.

In the 90's the magazine included a program disk.

Since the last issue in 1996, there was only one floppy disk in a DIN A4 cover.

In 1999, the last separate edition was published and was only made available for subscribers.

In the 80's there were a number of competitor magazines, such as "Happy Computer" (same publisher, but for all home computers), "Input 64" (Heise Verlag), "Magic Disk", "GameOn", "RUN" and a few more.

In addition to the monthly issues, there was also an extensive range of special issues.

These special editions (German) were mostly dedicated to a specific topic.

http://www.64er-online.de/download/sonderhefte/index.html

12.1.7 Retro Computer Scene Web-Drive

If you need to share or remotely archive your retro computer files, whether forever or for a limited period, don't fall back on those ugly sites covered in adverts, spam, expiry dates or trackers. Provided that you have access to a web browser you'll find it easy to get your files uploaded and shared using The Retro Computer Scenes webdrive, to Share, Archive or Link your retro computer files for use on your favourite forum, sites or even email them to your contacts using our custom email client. Enjoy access to our

Commodore 8bit disk-image manipulator to edit many popular disk images like .d64 .d71 .d81 and other CBM8bit file images.

Drag 'n' Drop a ".d64 .d71 .d80 .d81 .d82" Commodore disk-image into the box above to enjoy our disk image editor browser utility. Consider registering with an account in the cloud to share and save your images online. Your feedback is highly sought after for additional features. But for now, please enjoy!!

More to read can be found on the webpage: http://cbm8bit.com/webdrive/

12.1.8 Chris Huelsbeck Royalty-Free Music Vol. 1

https://chrishuelsbeck.bandcamp.com/album/royalty-free-music-vol-1

12.2 Communities / forums

12.2.1 Google Group

https://groups.google.com/forum/#!topic/comp.sys.cbm/v1qikTqAZZE

12.2.2 The Lemon Retro Forum

http://www.lemon64.com/forum/index.php

12.2.3 Forum64 (German)

https://www.forum64.de/

12.2.4 THEC64 community

http://thec64community.online/

12.3 Wikis

12.3.1 C64 Mini Wiki

This is an independent C64 Wiki that is hosted and filed by a single person.

https://gurce.net/c64mini/

12.3.2 C64 Wiki (German)

This is the most complete C64 related Wiki there is: https://www.c64-wiki.de/wiki/THEC64Mini

12.4 SID music

See also: 4.8 SID in stereo

12.4.1 High Voltage SID Collection

See also: 10.3.5 Gamesbase64

The High Voltage SID Collection (HVSC) is a freeware hobby project which organizes Commodore 64 music (also known as SID music) into an archive for both musicians and fans alike. The work on the collection is done completely by the team and contributors' spare time. Not to mention it is proudly one of the largest and most accurate computer music collections known.

For more info, please read the Info and FAQ sections of this site. Thank you.

12.4.2 Commodore SID 6581 Datasheet

See also: 4.8 SID in stereo

On this page you will find nearly everything that is known on hardware specifications for the SID 6581 Chip.

https://www.waitingforfriday.com/?p=661

12.5 Facebook

See also: 12.6.4 Facebook

12.5.1 THEC64 Mini group

https://www.facebook.com/groups/209280506324242/permalink/216680592250900/

12.5.2 The C64mini FANs Deutschland (German)

https://www.facebook.com/The-C64mini-FANs-Deutschland-423138851466241/

12.5.3 THEC64 Mini

https://www.facebook.com/c64mini/

12.6 Official pages

12.6.1 Homepage THEC64 Mini

https://thec64.com/

12.6.2 The Indiegogo Campaign Page

h t t p s : / / w w w . i n d i e g o g o . c o m / p r o j e c t s /
thec64-computer-and-games-console-computers#/

12.6.3 Twitter

https://twitter.com/thec64mini

12.6.4 Facebook

See also: 12.5 Facebook

https://www.facebook.com/THEC64computer/

12.6.5 Contact page

https://thec64.com/contact/

12.6.6 RetroGameDev

RetroGameDev was created to produce books, courses and support for the retro game development community. It will initially cover 8-bit hardware such as the Commodore 64, Nintendo Entertainment System, Sinclair ZX Spectrum and Sega Master System.

https://www.retrogamedev.com/

Here you will find a forum as well as books and software to download that deal with programming.

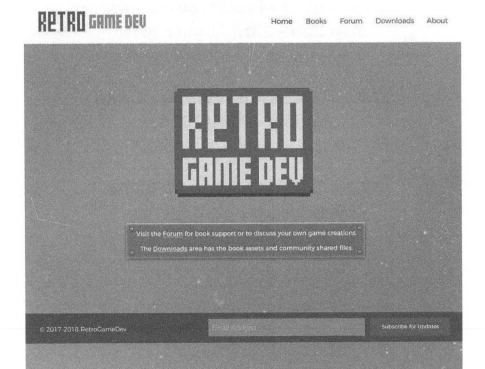

12.7 THEC64 Mini videos

This is the Retro Games' main YouTube page: https://www.youtube.com/channel/UC-lvVA19BR7PduUMeOXETOA

12.7.1 The C64 Mini – Announcement Trailer

https://www.youtube.com/watch?v=hXr_5sVuCHc

12.7.2 Promotion Video C64 Mini

https://www.youtube.com/watch?v=3bwYMOZG7gw

12.7.3 An introduction to THEC64 Mini

https://www.youtube.com/watch?v=hOyqOD2MIeI

12.7.4 THE 64 – Prototype Hardware
In Action – 23rd August 2016

https://www.youtube.com/watch?v=Kx_IVFdbka8&feature=youtu.be

12.7.5 THEC64 Mini manufacturing
update – April 2018

https://www.youtube.com/watch?v=BDo574mA9MA

12.7.6 THEC64 Mini and THEC64
Joystick Factory Production

https://www.youtube.com/watch?v=jLPYCfJJR7w

13 FAQ

Here you can find the official questions and answers of Retro Games Ltd. as well as additional ones from various forums and communities.

!ALWAYS install the newest firmware! This will solve usually many problems up front!

Question: I have more than 200 games on my stick. The carousel did not show all of them.
Answer: You can only add 100 games to the carousel.

Question: Do I lose my warranty if I open the case?
Answer: Yes, this would cause you to loss your warranty.

Question: Can I change the menu music?
Answer: The simple answer is No. But in principle, this is possible. Unfortunately, the music menu cannot be changed easily. This currently still implies a deep involvement in the system, see 7.1.1 UART Interface Root access and 7.1.3 Adding games to the carousel and changing the music.

Question: Every time I put the USB stick in my Mini, press the Power button, the Mini tries to run and shuts down after about 2 seconds. The Mini doesn't start.
Answer: This is most probably a power consumption problem. The Mini does not get enough power and shuts down because of this. Use a power supply with more power.

Question: The program I like to use for copying disk images to an USB pen drive is erased by my Anti-virus.
Answer: This was probably done as a "false positive". The Anti-virus software just guessed it wrong. There should be a possibility to put in a white list or declare it in some way as safe. Make sure the program comes from a reliable source!

Question: I can't see the .d64 file extension.
Answer: If you don't see ".d64" at the end of "thec64-drive8" or any other drive file, then you may have the filename extensions turned off in Windows.

Question: On some games the sound is delayed.
Answer: This seems to be a problem just with certain games. Perhaps a new firmware will fix this. But it can also be a problem due to video playback.

Question: I can't continue playing my Multi-Disk-Game when it asks for the second disk.
Answer: Try to put all files of the game in one single .d81 or .d82 which can hold more files. Use the DirMaster for this.

Question: When connected via HDMI my TV shows say "Not Supported" or "Resolution not supported".
Answer: Your TV is maybe too old to support the HMDI-Signal with the Mini. Also, the Mini now only supports PAL = 50Hertz. A NTSC = 60Hertz Version will come.

Question: Can I use an adapter or adapter cable for HDMI to DVI?
Answer: If your TV doesn't have an HDMI on it but has a DVI-I port, you might need to get a converter to convert the resolution for your TV's specific needs.

Question: Does the Mini work with a projector?
Answer: Yes. But you could have the same lag problem as using a TV or monitor.

Question: When trying to use my USB-stick I always get a "FILE NOT FOUND" Error.
Answer: Remove all files that are not a regular Commodore File format. Like .png .jpg .txt and so on. By now just .d64 or .d81.

Question: Some self-installed games come up with a hacker screen but there is no indication which key or button to press.
Answer: Most of the time you can continue by pressing a fire button either on port one or two, if not it's the space key.

Question: Why isn't <insert the name of your favourite C64 game here> included on THEC64 Mini?
Answer: A huge amount of time has been spent officially licensing the included games from their respective IP owners. Sadly, some IP rights prove to be excessively expensive to license and others are untraceable or too complex to untangle. We believe there is a good mix of game genres in the

supplied titles and all of them were highly rated upon original publication. There's definitely something for everyone!

Question: Can I attach <insert your favourite C64 peripheral here> to the Mini?
Answer: THEC64 Mini uses modern USB ports for attaching a keyboard, controllers and memory sticks. That unfortunately rules out connecting with any of the original C64 peripherals like cassette decks, disk drives, printers, cartridges and so on.

Question: Are there any two-player games included?
Answer: Yes. 24 of the supplied games can be two-player. 12 of those titles require two joysticks for a two-player game, while the other 12 can be played between two players using just one joystick and taking alternate goes. The remaining 40 supplied games are for one player. See thec64.com/games for details for each game.

Question: Can I buy a second joystick?
Answer: Yes. THEC64 Joystick can be purchased separately. Please check with any retailer that carries THEC64 Mini. Also see thec64.com/accessories.

Question: Does THEC64 joystick use micro switches?
Answer: No, THEC64 joystick uses tactile switches. However, if there is enough demand then we will certainly consider producing a joystick that uses micro switches in the future.

Question: Is the keyboard on THEC64 Mini functional?
Answer: No, it isn't. If a functional keyboard was to be included, the size of the Mini would have to be significantly larger to reproduce the original computer's keyboard. It was decided to include an on-screen virtual keyboard instead and allow full USB keyboards as well. Having said that, a full-size THEC64 is on the way and that does include a fully functional integral keyboard as part of the package. More about this you eventually will find on the THEC64 Main page.

Question: Can I add my own keyboard?
Answer: Yes. Connect an USB keyboard to the Mini while on the HOME screen. Specify your keyboard layout from a selection including UK, US, French, German, Spanish and Italian. Other layouts maybe added to the Mini in the future, via a firmware update.

Question: Can THEC64 Mini be upgraded?
Answer: There are no user-serviceable parts inside the Mini, but the firmware can be upgraded via the upgrade page. New features, changes in software and other improvements can be delivered using the 'System Information' option on the Mini and a downloaded firmware update file saved onto a FAT32 formatted USB memory stick.

Question: Can I load other games onto the Mini?
Answer: Currently, external files can be accessed via BASIC using a FAT32 formatted USB memory stick.

Question: Can an USB hub be used on THEC64 Mini?
Answer: It's impossible to guarantee that they will all work, but in general you should be able to connect an USB hub and use it on the Mini. We would recommend a powered hub (one that uses a separate power supply).

Question: Why am I seeing a delay between my joystick actions and the screen?
Answer: A number of HD TVs apply image processing to the image output from the Mini before displaying it on the screen. This introduces a slight delay, which makes it look like the games are slow to respond to your movements or pressing the button. There is nothing wrong with the Mini, the joystick or the TV. However, to reduce or eradicate this problem requires you to change the image processing options on your TV or engage 'Game Mode' on the TV. Please refer to the manual for your TV for further information.

Question: Can I use my own USB controller as well as – or instead of – THEC64 Joystick?
Answer: Yes, you can. We can't guarantee they all work but other USB controllers can be connected.

THEC64 Mini expects a controller to have a minimum of eight buttons. When you connect a controller, the Mini will attempt to automatically configure the controller, assigning the left FIRE, right FIRE, TL, TR, A, B, C and MENU buttons for you.

Typical USB gamepad shoulder buttons are usually assigned as left FIRE and right FIRE by the Mini. The SELECT button is typically assigned as button C and START becomes the MENU button, giving access to all of the expected menu options that the Mini needs. Most controllers will have their X and Y buttons as Mini's TL and TR buttons, leaving their A and B buttons to be A and B.

Having connected a USB controller to the Mini, it should only take a second or two for the Mini to register the controller. You can then use the controller to navigate the GAMES CAROUSEL and the OPTIONS windows on the HOME SCREEN and play games. When there are two control devices attached, either one can be used to navigate the screens and menus offered and to select and play games.

To further test an alternative USB controller, launch a game and check each button's functionality with the online instructions for the game found at www.thec64.com/games.

Question: Can I change how the Mini displays on my TV or monitor?
Answer: There are six different display modes available on the Mini. Pixel perfect, European 4:3 and North American 4:3. Each mode can then have a CRT filter applied, to match how the C64 games displayed on older TVs. You don't have to adjust any settings on your HD TV or monitor when switching between these display modes.

Question: Can I program on the Mini?
Answer: You have access to BASIC via the games carousel specifically to allow programming. Attach an USB keyboard to enhance the experience. Add an USB memory stick and you can also save and load your programs as well. See BASIC for more information.

Question: Why am I seeing a READONLY disk in BASIC when I have an USB memory stick connected?
Answer: Your USB memory stick isn't detected. There are a few possible explanations. The USB memory stick wasn't inserted before BASIC was launched from the GAMES CAROUSEL. Another explanation is that the memory stick isn't formatted to FAT32. A third possibility is that the memory stick is faulty. Memory sticks up to 64Gb have been tested and confirmed as working on the Mini, but it's not possible to test every single brand and size available. Please try a different memory stick. If you are using an USB hub, try accessing the memory stick by directly connecting it to the Mini, rather than using a hub. See BASIC for more information on programming in BASIC.

Question: Why isn't my THEC64-drive8.d64 file detected by BASIC?
Answer: Apart from the USB memory stick issues mentioned elsewhere in this FAQ, it could be because your file is incorrectly named, especially if you named the file on a Windows-based PC and don't have the file extensions shown. This could result in your file actually being named THEC64-drive8. d64.d64 (for example). Double-check that the name is correct by showing file extensions in Windows, so you can see the exact full name of the file before you try running it on the Mini.

Question: Do you use any Open Source code in the Mini?
Answer: Yes, we use some. You may obtain the corresponding Open Source code from us for a period of three years after our last shipment of this product, by sending a money order or cheque for 5 GBP to: GPL Compliance Division, Retro Games Ltd. Suite 112, Crystal House, New Bedford Road, Luton, England. LU1 1HS.

Please write "source for < firmware version number >" in the memo line of your payment.

Question: I need help playing one of the games supplied on the Mini!
Answer: Have you read the instructions at thec64.com/games? There are plenty of web sites that give hints and tips for playing the games included on the Mini. YouTube is also a very good source for tutorials and solutions.

Question: The joysticks have changed over when in a two player, two joystick game!
Answer: You just need to be aware that some games switch the joysticks on the Mini, so what would be player one's joystick becomes player two's joystick in a two player, two joystick game and vice versa.

Question: Why have some of the games been altered?
Answer: A small number of games have been slightly changed to improve your game playing experience when using the Mini. Any changes have been kept to an absolute minimum and have only been made when absolutely necessary. We have strived to keep the Mini as authentic as possible.

Question: I think I have found a problem on the Mini. How do I report it?
Answer: We always welcome feedback. To report a potential problem, please go to the Contact page and complete the online form. We will do our best to respond as quickly as possible.

Question: If I insert another USB stick it is not recognized or the Mini hangs up and stops.
Answer: Even if the USB ports of the Mini Plug&Play are Hot plug capable, the Mini should be restarted before switching to another USB stick. This may be solved in a future firmware update.

Question: Do USB2RS232 adapters work?
Answer: Yes. All of them should work.

Question: I found some games like Test drive, that will not run.
Answer: For some games, someone created M2I files so that they also can run on a SD2IEC. Defender OTC and Test drive are available.

Load M2I file into DirMaster and save as .d64

Try BASIC normally, if it still doesn't work try the following: First start the game "Creatures" from the carousel, leave it, load BASIC and run the game from there.

Question: I downloaded the multidisk and unpacked it as described and loaded it onto a stick under THEC64-drive8.d64 and tried to load with LOAD"$",8. But there was always an error message or the table of contents was empty (BASIC "List"). What did I do wrong?
Answer: Start a built-in game first, then go back to the main overview. Now load into BASIC and table of contents. Of course, do everything with an inserted stick.

Question: Some games want a joystick at port 1 but the C64 joystick is only accepted at port 2. What can be done?
Answer: Oh yes, this is definitely possible if you play a game on the Mini yourself, e.g. assign keys to the standard controller on port 2. With this you could use the joystick settings for the game to place the direction keys needed to control the game on the joystick at port 2 and if you can assign the fire buttons separately you can also place special functions (keys) from the game there. The game only needs to support keyboard control (which should be the case with Spy Hunter, for example). This would also solve the port 1 problem.

For others, there are some alterations necessary which you can find at https://freeze64.com/c64mini-hacks/. You can find them at the bottom in the section "JOYSTICK PORT 2 HACKS:".

Question: My Mini does not restart and I can only restart it when I disconnect the power plug. Is there another way?

Answer: In the unlikely event that the Mini stops responding when the power switch is turned off. Press and hold the switch for about six seconds to shut down the Mini. To turn the Mini back on, press and hold the power switch for two seconds until the power LED turns red.

Question: Can I pause a game?

Answer: Yes, this can be done by pressing the menu button on the THEC64 Joystick. The options menu is displayed and the game pauses during this time.

Question: Why can't the firmware binary have games injected into it?

Answer: A nice idea, but for that to accomplish you need to know exactly how the bin is created and where is which content. This maybe will be possible, when Retro Games releases the full source code.

Question: Some games are not showing up at my USB stick?

Answer: There is currently a display limit of 256 items (files and/or folders) on USB memory sticks per folder, including the root.

Files take priority over folders, so if you go over that item limit, files are always displayed in preference to folders.

For solving this out, this utility could be of a great help:

RomSort   https://github.com/jonthysell/RomSort/releases/download/v1.0.0.0/RomSort.1.0.zip - a small utility to sort a directory of files into alphabetical sub-directories. It could intelligently combine the smaller sub-directories.

Question: How do I make a cjm file?

Answer: Use one of these solutions:

"CJM Configurator for Windows" aka C64MiniLoaderCFG (Emanuele Bonin's windows app) https://drive.google.com/drive/folders/1G58teTaXt-6WuYjYW-5qAm67sJEFxA-9 and there c64MiniLoaderCFG_0064.zip

or "CJM Configuration File Tool online" Darkuni's web-based solution http://monroeworld.net/thread/56/thec64mini-configuration-file-official-thread

or   online   at   https://www.thec64minizone.com/cjm-configuration-file-tool/

Question: How do I create a cjm file for many games at once?

Answer: You can use this very simple batch script. David Walgrave shared his solution here: https://www.facebook.com/groups/209280506324242/permalink/313111392607819/

Put the games you want into one folder. Create a Default.cjm file in there that maps keys to your controller the way you want it. Then create the following batch script (haha just one line) in that folder too. It uses Default.cjm to create cjm files for every file in that folder.

Copy paste this and put it in a file like copycjm.bat

```
FOR I in (*.crt) DO echo F|xcopy Default.cjm
"~nI.cjm" /y
```

Note: you have to replace (*.crt) by (*.d64) or whatever file types you have in the folder :)

14 A wish list and answers from Retro Games

Options for Full top/bottom borders. So that on some programs that use sprites inside the top and bottom borders can be 100% visible. Take Galencia for example. On a C64C the sprites on the top + bottom borders can be seen in full. On the Mini, only half/less than half the sprites are displayed. I also have the same problem when playing games created with The Shoot Em Up Construction Kit. No score panel can be seen.

Retro Games: You cannot have full borders with HDMI 720p without shrinking the screen, which causes scaling objects. Only 240 C64 scan lines are available on a 720p screen (240 x 3 = 720). Hawkeye and Armelyte are two games found on the Mini that have border graphics and they display nicely without problems. The Mini shifts the screen up or down to bring the border graphics into view for these games. We may consider providing options to allow users to do this for their own programs.

Options for SID type. There are programs which have music designed for new SID as well as the old.

Retro Games: This could be a possibility.

Support for other file formats, tape and cartridge files would be great. And a proper interface for loading lose PRG and image files.

Retro Games: Other formats can be considered. However, TAP files are complicated as they require a user interface to control the cassette player (play, stop, rewind and so on).

An option to boot straight to BASIC, by passing the carousel. I don't need the included games. A firmware without carousel, just let it start in BASIC like a normal C64 - that's all I want. And if there must be a carousel, I wish the ability to exchange the games of it.

Retro Games: We may add the ability to boot into BASIC.

Support for a positional keyboard map, so we can use a Keyrah and a real C64 keyboard.

Retro Games: This is a possibility.

Use the keyboard to navigate the carousel and open the menu while in a game.

Retro Games: This is already in test and will be part of a future firmware upgrade.

Option to load your own choice of SID files in for playback on the carousel. **Optional dive noise emulation in BASIC** when loading/saving to disk images. **Full access to the VICE emulator settings.** Including the file browser and others.

Retro Games: Unfortunately, this cannot be taken into account at present. The primary focus is on user-friendliness in consideration to most of our customers and these wishes are still too particular.

Better joystick support: Support any HID joystick and let us re-map buttons.

Retro Games: A wide selection of joysticks should work already. We are considering how to allow users to re-map buttons.

I also like that you can remap the joystick buttons, including being able to run both virtual joysticks from a single gamepad. This makes it easier to use games like Spy Hunter, which uses the second joystick's fire button. I could also envision using all 6 buttons on an SNES gamepad for a single player game by mapping the d-pad and left bumper to stick 1 and the diamond and right bumper to stick 2.

Retro Games: Having a single controller/joystick mapped to both C64 joystick ports is currently not technically possible.

I'd like to see them upgrade to SDLVICE version 3.1, which has all that stuff built-in to the emulator in 8-bit style. That works much better in a self-contained emulator like this than the old WAMP interface.

Retro Games: The Mini user interface has been deliberately designed to meet the needs of the majority of users. Refer to the comments about usability and intended customers.

15 The handbook

This is the original Handbook text:

CARING FOR YOU AND THEC64 MINI

Please take a moment to read the following advice regarding THEC64 Mini computer:

CAUTION

- Do not connect cables while the Mini is powered on
- Only use a certified 5V/1A output AC adapter with an USB port
- Keep the Mini and all cables out of the reach from young children
- Do not position the Mini where it may cause someone to trip or stumble
- Do not power off the Mini while data is being loaded or saved. Do not expose the Mini to any of the following: liquids, high temperatures, high humidity, steam, direct sunlight, excessive dust or smoke
- Do not touch the Mini or connected cables during an electrical storm
- Do not allow small particles or any foreign objects to get inside the Mini
- Do not touch any of the connectors on the Mini

EPILEPSY INFORMATION

Some games might trigger symptoms in a small number of users who suffer from or are prone to epileptic seizures or blackouts, due to the rapid color-cycling and other graphical effects employed. These effects could trigger a previously undetected condition in people with no previous history of seizures or epilepsy.

Stop using the Mini immediately and consult a doctor if you or anyone using the Mini experiences dizziness, eye or muscle twitches, disorientation, affected vision, any involuntary movements, convulsions or seizures. Only resume after having sought medical advice.

To reduce the chances of experiencing symptoms associated with epilepsy:

- Use the Mini in a well-lit area and always keep a reasonable distance away from the TV or monitor screen

- Avoid prolonged use of the Mini. Take at least a fifteen-minute breaks after each hour of continuous play

- Avoid using the Mini when you are tired or need sleep

- Stop using the Mini immediately if you feel tired, experience discomfort or pain in your limbs or begin to feel ill

GETTING STARTED

Before connecting anything, check the contents of the packaging. You should have:

- THEC64 Mini Computer

- THEC64 Joystick (USB)

- HDMI Cable

- USB Power Supply Cable

Please make sure to use an AC adapter that has been approved for use in your country and read its instruction manual to ensure that it is able to supply power to this home computer.

THEC64 MINI

THEC64 Mini home computer is a compact, modern take on the classic home computer system that first appeared in 1982. The Mini is instantly reminiscent of the original design, although the keyboard is purely aesthetic and non-functional.

THEC64 Mini includes a virtual on-screen keyboard for selecting keys during a game. For most games that need access to a keyboard, this will be more than sufficient. THEC64 Mini can also connect to an USB keyboard, giving convenient access to all the keys when playing games or using the provided BASIC programming language.

SUSPENDING, EXITING, SAVING AND RESTORING

The computer provides handy options – via the MENU button on THEC64 Joystick – for suspending, exiting, saving and restoring. The original classic games provided with the Mini often include their own pause, save and load features. In most cases these will have no effect, so please use the MENU button functionality instead.

We have worked hard to reproduce the experience of playing the original games, including all of the features present in those games. Retro Games Limited cannot be held responsible for any errors found in the originally published games.

SETTING UP THEC64 MINI

1. Ensure that your TV or monitor is switched off before you connect THEC64 Mini

2. Connect one end of the HDMI cable into THEC64 Mini and then connect the other end to your TV or monitor

3. Connect THEC64 Joystick to either of THEC64 Mini's USB ports

4. Connect the supplied USB power cable into a suitable USB power source and then connect the other end to the micro-USB port on THEC64 Mini

5. THEC64 Mini automatically turns on and the Power LED glows red

6. Switch on your TV or monitor and choose the appropriate HDMI input source. You will see THEC64 Mini's Region screen*

7. Now choose your preferred language for THEC64 Mini. Having selected, press the MENU button on THEC64 joystick to confirm your choice

8. From THEC64 Mini HOME screen, choose a game to play from the games carousel

9. To turn THEC64 Mini off, press the power switch. This places THEC64 Mini into a shutdown state

10. To turn THEC64 Mini back on from shutdown, press and hold the power switch for a few seconds until the Power LED glows red again *THEC64 Mini will remember your region choice and use it automatically from now on. To change it later, see the OPTIONS below the games carousel

PLAYING GAMES

Use THEC64 Joystick to select a title from the on-screen games carousel and then press either FIRE button to load. Once in the game, start playing by pressing TL on the joystick. If that doesn't work for a particular game, press either FIRE button instead.

THEC64 JOYSTICK

THEC64 Joystick has eight buttons, referred to as left FIRE, right FIRE, TL, TR, A, B, C and MENU.

The joystick is used to:

(i) Highlight and select items in the Mini's games carousel or from various other menus and screens (using the directional stick and the left or right FIRE buttons)

(ii) Play the games

Please regularly visit www.thec64.com for full game instructions, an expanded user manual, user forums, updates and firmware upgrades!

16 Acknowledgements & bibliographies

This "Thank you list" shows contributors that were so nice to let me use some text they provided for this book. Sometimes as a chapter or as a text passage.

Retro Games: Thank you for many different things.

Gurce (Webmaster and owner of http://gurce.net); UART Interface for serial Root access; Compatible Hardware; Replacing the Kernal and 1541 DOS ROM; U-Boot-Trick

Spannernick (Moderator of the thec64community.online); Root Access / FEL Mode; How to use D81 D82

Artur Gadawski (Owner of www.7-bit.pl, retro.7-bit.pl) UART Interface; USB 2 D-Sub Adapter rys_mkii

Anthony Jordan (RiotRetroGaming on https://www.facebook.com/RiotRetroGaming/)

Frank Buss (http://www.frank-buss.de/c64/) C64 USB Joystick Adapter

Jan Janssen (http://www.c-64.org/de/os.html) Operation Systems

Marcus Gritsch: Competition Pro Retro Joystick USB Adapter

Stefan Blixth: JoyDivision Joystick Adapter

Markus Egger: THEC64 Disker (https://www.facebook.com/m.m.egger)

Spinal: Arduino Joystick (http://thec64community.online/user/11)

Stuart Duncan: Linux-Sunxi

Alan Hammerton: MiniMount (http://www.retro-now.com/minimount-play-d64-images-on-thec64-mini-more-easily)

Chris Bruce: ACE (http://csbruce.com/cbm/ace/)

Additional thanks for some Text elements to:

Richard/TND (Webmaster of http://tnd64.unikat.sk)

C64Mini FEL-mode hack - no UART needed – by jj0 Jeroen

17 Legal code

All changes, adjustments, hardware or software are at your own risk and legal responsibility. I assume no liability in any aspect!

Disclaimer (Disclaimer)

Based on: eRecht24.de

Liability for contents

The contents of this book have been prepared with the greatest care. However, I cannot assume any liability for the correctness, completeness and relevance of the contents.

Liability for links

This book contains links to external websites of third parties, whose contents I have no influence over. Therefore, I cannot guarantee the contents. The respective provider or operator of the pages is always responsible for the contents of the linked pages. The linked pages were checked for possible legal infringements at the time of being added to this book. Illegal contents were not recognizable at the time of addition. However, permanent monitoring of the content of the linked pages is unreasonable without concrete evidence of a violation of the law. Upon notification of violations of the law, such links will be removed immediately.

Copyright

The contents and works created by the site operators on these pages are subject to German copyright law. Duplication, editing, distribution and any kind of use outside the limits of copyright law require the written consent of the respective author or creator. Downloads and copies of this site are only permitted for private, non-commercial use. As far as the contents on these sites were not created by the operator, the copyrights of third parties are respected. In particular, the contents of third parties are marked as such. Should you nevertheless become aware of a copyright infringement, please inform us accordingly. As soon as we become aware of any such infringements, we will remove such content immediately.

The use of the contact data published within the scope of the imprint obligation by third parties for sending unsolicited advertising and information material is hereby expressly prohibited. The operators of these pages particularly reserve the right to take legal action in the event of unsolicited advertising information being sent, for example in the form of spam mails.

Severability Clause

If sections or individual terms of this statement are not legal or correct, the content or validity of the other parts remain uninfluenced by this fact.